SERIES EDITORS

TRACY L. PELLETT   JACK RUTHERFORD   CLAUDIA BLACKMAN

Skills, Drills & Strategies for

Badminton

Donald C. Paup
The George Washington University

Bo Fernhall
The George Washington University

Holcomb Hathaway, Publishers
Scottsdale, Arizona 85250

Library of Congress Cataloging-in-Publication Data

Paup, Donald C.
    Skills, drills & strategies for badminton / Donald C. Paup, Bo Fernhall.
      p.   cm. — (The teach, coach, play series)
    Includes index.
    ISBN 1-890871-12-5
    1. Badminton (Game) I. Title: Badminton. II. Title: Skills, drills, and strategies for
badminton. III. Fernhall, Bo. IV. Title. V. Series.

GV1007 .P28 2000
796.345—dc21

                                        99-056784

 Holcomb Hathaway, Publishers
6207 North Cattle Track Road, Suite 5
Scottsdale, Arizona 85250
(480) 991-7881
www.hh-pub.com

10 9 8 7 6 5 4 3 2 1

ISBN 1-890871-12-5

Printed in the United States of America.

Contents

iii

SECTION 3   Skills and Drills   17

(Drills fall within each Skill section)

Preface

The books in the *Teach, Coach, Play* series emphasize a systematic learning approach to sports and activities. Both visual and verbal information are presented so that you can easily understand the material and improve your performance.

Built-in learning aids help you master each skill in a step-by-step manner. Using the cues, summaries, skills, drills, and illustrations will help you build a solid foundation for safe and effective participation now and in the future.

This text is designed to illustrate correct techniques and demonstrate how to achieve optimal results. Take a few minutes to become familiar with the textbook's organization and features. Knowing what to expect and where to look for material will help you get the most out of the textbook, your practice time, and this course.

Your needs are changing, your courses are changing, your students are changing, and the demands from your administration are changing. By setting out to create a series of books that addresses many of these changes, we've created a series that:

- Provides complete, consistent coverage of each sport—the basics through skills and drills to game strategies so you can meet the needs of majors and non-majors alike.
- Includes teaching materials so that new and recently assigned instructors have the resources they need to teach the course.
- Allows you to cover exactly the sports and activities you want with the depth of coverage you want.

What's in the *Teach, Coach, Play* Series?

- Nine activities:
    Skills, Drills, & Strategies for Badminton
    Skills, Drills, & Strategies for Basketball
    Skills, Drills, & Strategies for Bowling
    Skills, Drills, & Strategies for Golf

Skills, Drills, & Strategies for Racquetball
Skills, Drills, & Strategies for Strength Training
Skills, Drills, & Strategies for Swimming
Skills, Drills, & Strategies for Tennis
Skills, Drills, & Strategies for Volleyball
- Accompanying Instructor's Manuals

What's in the Student *Teach, Coach, Play* Textbooks?

The basic approach in all of the *Teach, Coach, Play* activity titles is to help students improve their skills and performance by building mastery from simple to complex levels.

The basic organization in each textbook is as follows:

Section 1 overviews history, organizations and publications, conditioning activities, safety, warm-up suggestions, and equipment.

Section 2 covers exercises or skills, participants, action involved, rules, facility or field, scoring, and etiquette.

Section 3 focuses on skills and drills or program design.

Section 4 addresses a broad range of strategies specifically designed to improve performance now and in the future.

Section 5 provides a convenient glossary of terms.

Supplements to Support You and Your Students

The *Teach, Coach, Play* books provide useful and practical instructional tools. Each activity is supported by its own manual. Each of these instructor's manuals includes classroom management notes, safety guidelines, teaching tips, ideas for inclusion of students with special needs, drills, lesson plans, evaluation notes, test bank, and a list of resources for you.

About the Authors

Donald C. Paup, Ph.D., is a Professor and Director of Exercise Science Programs in the Department of Prevention and Community Health in the School of Public Health and Health Services at The George Washington University in Washington, D.C. Dr. Paup is a past U.S. national men's doubles and mixed doubles champion and served as captain and coach of Thomas Cup and Uber Cup teams. He is a member of the Badminton Hall of Fame and recipient of the Ken Davidson Sportsmanship Award. As an administrator, Dr. Paup served on the NASPE and AIAW Intercollegiate Badminton Sport Committees, was Tournament Director for two AIAW National Championships, and was a USBA Director from 1976 to 1982. Dr. Paup has taught numerous badminton camps and workshops in recent years and coaches the GWU badminton team.

Bo Fernhall, Ph.D., is a Professor of Exercise Science in the Department of Prevention and Community Health in the School of Public Health and Health Services at The George Washington University in Washington, D.C. He played competitive badminton at the national level for ten years and is a former Connecticut state singles champion. Dr. Fernhall has also taught badminton at the college level.

Preliminaries

Although the New York Badminton Club, founded in 1879, became the first organized badminton club in the world, historical evidence indicates that games somewhat like badminton were played in ancient Greece, in the fifth century in Asia, and in the thirteenth century in Europe. These games became known as battledore and shuttlecock and used some sort of feathered projectile that was kicked or struck with a hitting implement. During the years between 1850 and 1870, battledore and shuttlecock evolved into the sport of badminton in both India and England. In India, the game was called *poona,* and the first rules were written in the early 1870s. The game took the name of badminton after being played at Badminton House, the Duke of Beaufort's estate in Gloucestershire (Avon), England. The game became popular among English army officers who served in both countries around that time.

The English Badminton Association was founded in 1893 and brought 14 clubs together under a common set of laws (rules); this is believed to be the first badminton association. Badminton quickly spread throughout the British Isles. Competitive badminton began in 1898 when the first open competition was held. The next year the All England Championships were held. Today this tournament continues to be one of the most prestigious badminton events in the world. By 1901 the "Laws of Badminton" were developed with a standard **court** size, shuttlecock construction, and rules of play, which have changed very little over the years. The *Badminton Gazette* became the first badminton magazine in 1907 and is still published today. Badminton grew rapidly between 1900 and 1930, and the **International Badminton Federation (IBF)** was founded by 9 national organizations. The IBF has grown to 140 members as of 1999. With the rapid growth and popularity of badminton in the United States, the American Badminton Association (ABA) was founded in 1936. In 1977 the ABA became the U.S. Badminton Association and is now **USA Badminton.** The first national championships were held in April 1937 in Chicago.

Age-group championships began in 1947 with the U.S. National Junior Championships. Junior competition now includes the following divisions: Under 21, 18, 16, 14, and 12. Senior competition at the national level includes ages from 35 years up to 80+ at 5-year intervals. Badminton has been contested at the collegiate level for women since 1969 and for men since 1975. Although badminton is not an official NCAA sport, it has received the status of an emerging NCAA sport, a classifi-

HISTORY OF THE GAME

court The area marked by boundary lines for playing badminton.

International Badminton Federation (IBF) Governing body for international competition.

USA Badminton The national governing body for badminton in the United States.

cation allowing women's collegiate competition in new sports to increase gender equity. If badminton competition grows to 50 percent representation of NCAA schools, an official NCAA championship could be offered.

The world team championships for men, the **Thomas Cup** (badminton equivalent to the Davis Cup in tennis), was first held in 1948 and is now a biennial event. The world team championship for women, the **Uber Cup,** followed in 1956. The U.S. men placed second in 1952, and the U.S. women held the Uber Cup from 1959 to 1965. Badminton was held as a trial sport in the 1972 Olympic Games in Munich, Germany; was played as a demonstration sport in the 1988 Olympic Games in Seoul, South Korea; and became a full medal sport in the 1992 Olympic Games in Barcelona, Spain. In the 1996 Centennial Olympic Games held in Atlanta, **mixed doubles** became the fifth badminton event. Players from China, Denmark, Indonesia, Korea, and Malaysia were the primary medal winners.

Badminton has struggled in recent years as a minor sport in the United States. Competitive badminton requires an indoor facility with a 26-foot-high ceiling. Although badminton is a very popular sport in high school and for college activities courses, scheduling of gymnasiums is difficult when trying to compete for the same space used by basketball, volleyball, and indoor soccer. Now that badminton is an Olympic sport, it is anticipated that there will be more publicity and awareness of the sport in the United States than in the past. We hope young male and female athletes will look to the sport for fun, fitness, and competition. With the small number of tournament players in the United States, a good athlete who is dedicated to the sport has a much better chance to play in national and international competition than an athlete of almost any other sport. Table 1.1 lists important dates in badminton history.

Thomas Cup An international men's team competition held every 2 years.

Uber Cup An international women's team competition held every 2 years.

mixed doubles A game contested with a male and a female on each team.

TABLE 1.1 Important badminton dates.

YEAR	EVENT
1873	The sport of badminton established in England and India
1879	New York Badminton Club, first in the world, founded
1893	English Badminton Association, first association in the world, founded
1899	First All England Badminton Championship held, with winner traditionally considered world champion
1903	First international competition, contested between England and Ireland in Dublin
1907	*Badminton Gazette*, first badminton journal, published
1934	IBF, governing body of international badminton, founded
1936	ABA, governing body of badminton in the U.S., founded
1937	First U.S. National Championships held, Chicago
1947	First U.S. National Junior Championships held
1948	Thomas Cup, international team competition for men, started
1956	Uber Cup, international team competition for women, started
1969	First Intercollegiate badminton championship for women held, New Orleans, LA
1975	First Intercollegiate badminton championship for men held, Toledo, OH
1977	WBF founded; governs world badminton championships, on alternate years to Thomas Cup
1977	ABA changed name to USBA; offered individual memberships
1981	First World Games held, included first participation by People's Republic of China in open international competition, San Jose, CA
1989	Sudirman Cup, world mixed team championship, established
1992	Badminton full medal sport in Olympic Games, Barcelona, Spain
1996	Mixed doubles a medal event in Olympic Games, Atlanta, GA

The primary organizations associated with badminton:

Asian Badminton Confederation
101 Cecil Street #16-01
Tong Eng Building
Singapore 0106

The Badminton Association of England
National Badminton Centre
Bradwell Road
Loughton Lodge
Milton Keynes MK8 9LA
England
www.intbadfed.org

Badminton Canada
1600 James Naismith Drive
Gloucester, Ontario, K1B 5N4
Canada
www.badminton.ca

International Badminton Federation
4 Manor Park
Mackenzie Way
Cheltenham, Gloucestershire
GL519TU UK
www.intbadfed.org

United Kingdom
Phone +44 1242 234904
Fax +44 1242 21030

USA Badminton
One Olympic Plaza
Colorado Springs, CO 80909
Phone (719) 578-4808
Fax (719) 578-4507
www.usabadminton.org

Asian Badminton
Asian Badminton Confederation
101 Cecil Street #16-01
Tong Eng Building
Singapore 0106

Badminton Canada
Badminton Canada
1600 James Naismith Drive
Gloucester, Ontario
K1B 5N4, Canada
www.badminton.ca

Badminton Now
The Badminton Association of England
National Badminton Centre
Bradwell Road, Loughton Lodge
Milton Keynes MK8 9LA, England

Badminton USA
USA Badminton
One Olympic Plaza
Colorado Springs, CO 80909
www.usabadminton.org

Official Rules of Play (USBA Handbook)
USA Badminton
One Olympic Plaza
Colorado Springs, CO 80909
www.usabadminton.org

World Badminton
International Badminton Federation
4 Manor Park
Mackenzie Way, Cheltenham
Gloucestershire, England GL51 9TX
www.intbadfed.org

General Conditioning

When badminton players are of equal skill, whether novice or advanced, fitness becomes an important factor in deciding the winner. Endurance is important because badminton matches generally last between 30 and 90 minutes, of which 30 percent to 45 percent of the total time on court is actual competition. Most **rallies** are between 4 and 10 seconds in duration and consist of play patterns characterized by abrupt changes in direction coupled with explosive jumping and lunging. The time

rally The exchange of shots during play or during warm-up.

racket An implement used to strike the shuttle.

shuttle (bird, shuttlecock) The object hit back and forth over the net.

clear (lob) A shot hit high and deep to the opponent's backcourt.

smash The primary attacking shot, hit with maximal, or near maximal, velocity and power and with a steep downward angle.

drive A sidearm stroke hit so as to land between the opponent's short service line and the back boundary line.

backhand A stroke hit on the opposite side of the body from the racket hand (e.g., left side of the body for right-handed players).

supination The outward rotation of the forearm, primarily used in backhand strokes.

pronation The inward rotation of the forearm, primarily used in forehand strokes.

footwork Techniques of foot movement patterns in moving about the court.

shot A clear, drive, drop, or smash that has been hit from one of the stroking positions.

between rallies averages about 8 seconds. Strength is also an important factor in badminton even though the **rackets** weigh less than 4 ounces. Men and women can smash the **shuttle** at speeds up to 210 mph and 180 mph, respectively, and many **clears, smashes,** and **drives** are struck with near-maximum effort, especially on the **backhand.** In addition, leg strength is important for lunging to the net and jumping backward in the court to hit clears and smashes. Players who are in excellent physical condition develop confidence and feel comfortable playing long rallies that require a great deal of running, jumping, and lunging.

To increase stamina, strength, and speed, the fitness training program for badminton players must consist of drills and play behaviors that are based on the following two major physiological conditioning principles: (1) the overload principle—to increase fitness, conditioning work levels must be greater than the player's current exertion levels; (2) the law of specificity—the exercise movement patterns used during conditioning must simulate actual play patterns used in competition. Thus, endurance, strength, and quickness will increase for the movement patterns used in the sport.

Three general categories of fitness training programs, which are based upon the demands of the sport and the physiological principles described above, should be followed; these are (1) traditional fitness training, (2) shadow drills, and (3) pressure training.

Traditional Fitness Training

Traditional training methods include wind sprints, running, rope skipping, circuit weight training, and calisthenics. Five specific examples are listed below.

1. Wind sprints of 80–90 yards at full speed; 6–8 sets (bouts) of very high-intensity exercise; 10-second exercise periods with 30-second recovery period
2. 6–8 sets of relatively high-intensity exercise; 30-second exercise period with 60-second recovery period
   - Wind sprints at 90–95 percent maximum speed (200–240 yards)
3. 3–5 sets of moderate-intensity exercise; 1- to 3-minute exercise period with 2-minute recovery period
   - Running at about 85–90 percent maximum speed (400–800 yards)
4. 1 set of continuous aerobic exercise (run/cycle/jump rope); 10–60 minutes at 70–85 percent maximum heart rate (subtract your age in years from 220 and multiply by .70 to get training heart rate for this exercise; for a 17-year-old, the training heart rate would be .70(220 – 17) = 142 beats/minute)
5. Weight training or circuit weight training, using various machines (Universal Gym, Nautilus) or free weights to work trunk, lower-body, and upper-body major muscle groups
   - 1–3 sets of 8–12 repetitions lifting about 70–80 percent of 1-RM (heaviest weight that can be lifted one time) to provide general overall body strength
   - After about six weeks of training, lifting heavier weight at fewer repetitions (2–4 sets of 3–5 repetitions lifting about 90 percent of 1-RM)

Badminton players should emphasize toe raises, leg flexion and extension, trunk flexion and extension, triceps extension, **supination** (outward rotation) and **pronation** (inward rotation) of the forearm, and wrist and shoulder exercises.

Shadow Drills

Shadow drills are running and jumping exercises designed to simulate play patterns and improve balance, **footwork,** and court speed as well as fitness. For maximum benefit, the player should carry a badminton racket and simulate the execution of a badminton **shot** at each court position. Shadow drills use the same time periods as wind sprints (10-second drill/30-second rest; 30-second drill/60-second rest; 1- to 3-minute drill/2- 3-minute rest).

1. Nondirected shadow drills are conducted by the player running from the **base** position to the six primary areas on the court, as shown in Figure 1.1.
   - Single-position drills: The player moves back and forth from the base position to one of six court positions (i.e., base to 2 [right **forecourt**]).
   - Two-position drills: The player moves back and forth from base to two court positions (i.e., base to 1 [left forecourt] to base to 4 [right **backcourt**]) for diagonal court coverage. Base to 3 to base to 6 is a side-to-side pattern.
   - Multiple-position drills: The player moves back and forth from base to various court positions in a set pattern or in random order.

Once players have learned basic footwork and movement patterns, self-directed shadow drills can be performed in gymnasium space that does not have badminton court lines. Thus, small unmarked areas of the gym can be effectively used for fitness training and movement pattern instruction.

2. Directed shadow drills are conducted as the player moves back and forth from base to court positions 1 to 6 as directed by the instructor, who is positioned at the center forecourt facing the player (Figure 1.2).
   - The instructor uses hand signals to direct the player about the court at as fast a rate as the player can attain while maintaining good balance. In more advanced directed shadow drills, the instructor signals the player's movement position by calling out a number (i.e., 5 indicates movement to left backcourt position).

base A ready position to which players try to return after each shot.

forecourt The area between the net and the center of the court.
backcourt The area between the center and the back boundary of the court.

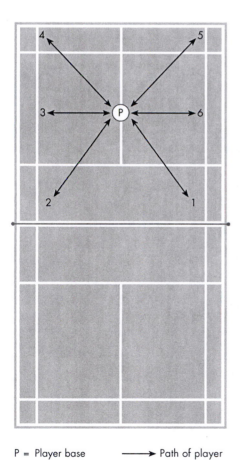

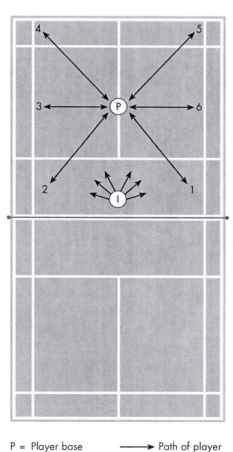

Figure 1.1 (on left)
Shadow drill positions showing movement to the four corners and two sides from the base position and the return.

Figure 1.2 (on right)
Shadow drill with the instructor or another player directing movements to the various positions.

P = Player base   ⟶ Path of player

P = Player base   ⟶ Path of player
I = Instructor

drop shot (drop) A shot hit from any position that passes close to the net and lands in the opponent's front court (in front of the short service line).

Pressure Training

These are continuous, high-intensity badminton playing drills that require the player to move to all areas of the court either in set patterns or in variations to return a shuttle hit by the instructor or another player.

1. Two-position pressure training drill: Figure 1.3 shows a movement pattern in which player A hits all net **drop shots** and must alternate runs from the backcourt to the forecourt for each shot. Player B, the setter, alternates hitting shots deep and at the net so player A has to work hard to retrieve the shuttle.
   - Multiple-position pressure training drill: Player A must retrieve the shuttle from any court position (1–6) with a shot hit to player B in a specified court area (i.e., position 4), as shown in Figure 1.4. Positions 3 and 6 are not targets for player A in this drill.
2. Two-on-one pressure training drill: In this drill, players B and C can hit the shuttle to anyplace on the court with the objective of making player A move at top speed to return the shuttle (Figure 1.5). Player A can hit any shot as well. This format is useful for 30- to 60-second work intervals. If a shuttle is missed, another one is immediately put in play by player B. Thus, each rally is essen-

---

Figure 1.3

In the two-position pressure training drill, player A runs back and forth from the net to the backcourt and hits all drop shots. Player B plays in the forecourt and alternates hitting clears and drops.

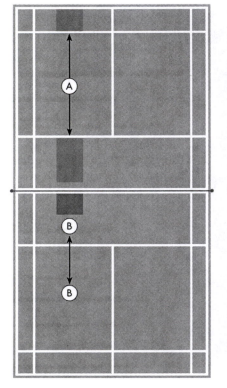

→ Path of player

Figure 1.4

Multiple-position pressure training drill with player A hitting all shots to player B in court position 4.

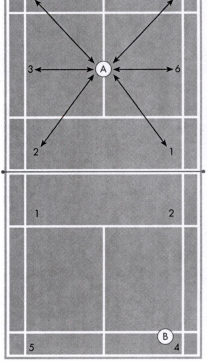

→ Path of player

Figure 1.5

Two-on-one pressure training drill.

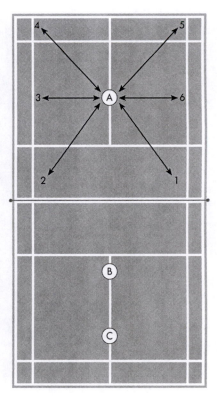

→ Path of player

tially a 30- to 60-second rally. The players will then rotate positions after each rally for a less intense rest interval.

Effective fitness training programs for badminton should include combinations of the above types of activities performed at the prescribed intensities and durations. The pressure training fitness programs become more effective as the player's skill increases to a level where long rallies can be played without making an error.

WARM-UP AND COOL DOWN

Warm-up for badminton consists of low-intensity exercise with gradually increasing activity over a period of 3 to 5 minutes until the player begins to sweat. Stretching exercises can be introduced at this time to increase or maintain player flexibility. The player can then do calisthenics, lunges, jumps, and racket-swinging exercises. These activities can be done off the court. Once the player moves onto the court, the warm-up consists of skill activities in which the player hits a variety of clears, drops, and smashes with power and accuracy.

Stretching exercises are recommended following a hard workout or competition to maintain or improve flexibility and/or prevent muscle soreness. Stretching exercises can *also* be done as the last portion of the warm-up if the player has low flexibility or is recovering from an injury. One to three sets of static stretching (no bobbing) of 20- to 30-second duration is recommended.

A typical workout for badminton should include the activities and approximate time periods listed in Table 1.2.

TABLE 1.2   A typical workout for badminton.

Warm-up	3–5 minutes
Stretching (optional)	5–7 minutes
Calisthenics, lunges, jumps, racket swinging	5–15 minutes
Pressure training, drills, game situations	30–90 minutes
Cool down	5–10 minutes
Stretching	5–10 minutes
Approximate total workout	1–2 hours

EQUIPMENT

Footwear

Badminton shoes are primarily sold in Asian countries. The badminton shoe is very light in weight, has good heel cushion, and is very flexible. Most players wear volleyball or racquetball shoes or some of the lighter tennis shoes. The shoes should be nonmarking and have good gripping (treads) to allow for quick starts and changes in direction. Shoes with greater cushioning may be desired for large people or when playing on concrete or other hard surfaces.

Clothing

Badminton clothing consists of lightweight shorts and shirts for men and shorts or skirts and shirts or tennis dresses for women. Although competitive badminton used to require all-white clothing, pastel colors and matching outfits in good taste are often worn by partners and members of badminton teams. School gym attire is worn for school badminton classes.

Headbands are often worn by players to help keep hair and sweat out of their eyes. Wrist sweatbands are used to keep sweat from dripping into the hand. Racket handles that get wet often become very slippery. A racket that slips out of a player's hand could cause serious injury to another player or spectator. Drying a racket handle with a towel and using rosin help to keep the **grip** from becoming too slippery to hold. In addition, new racket grips can be purchased at most sporting goods stores for about $5.

Goggles

Protective eyewear is recommended for students in badminton classes. This is especially important where there are a large number of novice players, some of whom have great power but little racket control. Players seldom get hit with a racket, but an eye injury (detached retina) could occur from a smash hit at close range, especially when players are only a few feet apart in the forecourt. Protective goggles should be constructed of polycarbonate, a material that will not break or shatter in the eye if hit by a racket or shuttle.

Implements

There are a variety of shuttlecocks and rackets used for badminton.

Shuttlecocks

The shuttlecocks, more commonly called **birds** or shuttles, are made from goose feathers (14–16 feathers inserted into a leather-covered cork base) or nylon and weigh between 73 and 85 grains (4.74–5.50 grams; 1/6th ounce). Plastic shuttles have poor durability and flight characteristics and are not recommended for school, club, or tournament use. Most schools use nylon shuttles because their durability is about ten times that of feather shuttles, although feather shuttles have better flight characteristics. Shuttle speed is important and can be tested by hitting the shuttle with a full underhand stroke from one **back boundary line** toward the other. Shuttles of proper speed should land within a 9-inch area on either side of the long service line for **doubles** (see Figure 1.6). Proper shuttle speed is necessary because it makes the game one of finesse rather than brute power. Shuttles falling outside this range can be corrected to proper speed by tipping feathers inward (to speed up) or outward (to slow down).

Shuttle care is important because proper humidification greatly increases the longevity of both feather and nylon shuttles. A damp paper towel can be inserted into a tube of shuttles about 2 hours before play to humidify shuttles. This is especially important in dry climates and during the winter.

Rackets

Badminton rackets are made from various blends of aluminum, steel, and carbon-graphite-boron compositions. Racket length cannot exceed 26¾ inches; the head is limited to an 11-inch by 9-inch length and width. They weigh between 90 and 110 grams, or about 3½ ounces. The rackets have an eight-sided handle covered with a leather or synthetic grip.

Strings are generally made of synthetic nylon and range between 20 and 22 gauge. Stringing tension is generally between 15 and 20 pounds. Rackets strung at high tension (near 20 pounds) have greater power and "feel" but reduced durability. Individual strings, if broken, can be replaced without having to use a stringing machine. Badminton requires a modest investment in equipment. Dealers who specialize in selling badminton equipment advertise in USBA publications (discussed earlier). Write to the USBA for a list of advertisers in your area of the country.

grip *The covering, usually leather, of the racket handle; the positioning of the hand holding the racket handle.*

bird (shuttle, shuttlecock) *A slang term for a shuttle or shuttlecock, which is the object hit back and forth over the net.*

back boundary line (baseline) *The end boundary of the court; also called the long service line for singles.*

doubles *A game played with two players on each side.*

Figure 1.6

A shuttle with correct speed should land within 9 inches of the long service line for doubles when hit with a full swing from the opposite back boundary line.

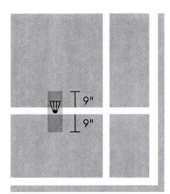

The Game

GENERAL DESCRIPTION

Badminton is a racket sport that can be enjoyed by just about anyone because it is easy to learn and can be played at any level. It is probably one of the few games where a player can learn the basics and actually play a game with some level of proficiency in the same day. However, it is very difficult to master the game and to play at a highly competitive level, and only a few players progress to this point. Although badminton can be enjoyed outdoors, competitive play and most recreational play take place indoors since wind and other environmental factors will affect the flight of the shuttle. The object of the game is to hit the shuttle over the net with enough control to make it land in the court on the other side of the net. The opposing player then attempts to return the shuttle over the net before it touches the floor because the shuttle is not allowed to bounce and must be played in the air before it hits the floor. The rally continues until a player is unable to return the shuttle into the other court. This makes for a very fast game; at a highly competitive level, badminton is the fastest of all the racket sports.

SKILLS INVOLVED

A badminton player must learn the fundamental racket **strokes** used in the game in order to execute the basic shots. These strokes can be separated into eight groups:

1. **Overhead** forehand stroke
2. Overhead backhand stroke
3. **Underhand** forehand stroke
4. Underhand backhand stroke
5. Sidearm forehand stroke
6. Sidearm backhand stroke
7. Blocking strokes
8. Service stroke

stroke The basic hitting pattern from which all shots are executed.

overhead Strokes hit above head height.

underhand A stroke in which the shuttle is contacted below the waist and in front of the body.

baseline (back boundary line) The back boundary line of the court.

half-court shot A shot hit down the sideline that lands in the opponent's court midway between the net and the back baseline.

block shot A soft return of a smash requiring very little racket motion.

defense A situation in which the opponent has the opportunity to hit a smash.

offense A player or team that is on the attack or that has the opportunity to smash.

service The act of putting the shuttle into play to begin a rally.

short serve A serve hit just over the net to land near the short service line; used as the primary serve in doubles.

flick serve A service hit with a trajectory to just pass over the receiver's outstretched racket and land near the long service line.

drive serve A hard and quickly hit service with a flat trajectory.

On both the forehand and backhand sides, the following three overhead strokes can be performed in a variety of ways in order to execute different types of shots:

1. Defensive and offensive clears—deep shots designed to land just inside the opponent's **baseline**
2. Slow and quick drops—shots designed to land close to the net
3. Smashes—high-speed shots designed to hit the floor as fast as possible

The underhand strokes are used to execute the following two shots:

1. Drops
2. Clears

The sidearm strokes are very versatile and, depending on the skill of the player, are used for the following four shots:

1. Defensive and offensive clears
2. Slow and fast drop shots
3. Hard drives—line-drive–type shots designed to hit the shuttle to a spot as fast as possible
4. **Half-court shots**—half-speed shots designed to first clear the net and land halfway between the net and the baseline (used mostly in doubles)

The **block shots** are used mostly on **defense,** to block a hard shot back into the opponent's court. They are also used on **offense,** primarily in doubles. The **services** are very important strokes because each point starts with a serve, and (like volleyball) a point can only be earned while serving. There are three basic types of serves:

1. High deep serves—designed to land just inside the opponent's baseline
2. Low **short serves**—designed to land just over the opponent's short service line
3. **Flick serves** and **drive serves**—designed to quickly flick the shuttle over the opponent's head or drive the shuttle past the opponent

Because badminton is such a fast game, quick reflexes and physical conditioning are also necessary. It is not unusual for well-conditioned players to beat players with better skills, simply by keeping the play going and tiring out their opponents. Thus, shot making must be combined with a strenuous physical conditioning program in order to become a successful badminton player. Finally, a clear understanding of playing strategy is needed. It does not help to have good shots and be in excellent physical condition if the player cannot hit the right shot at the right time.

PARTICIPANTS

game A badminton game is played to 15 points in all events except women's singles, which is played to 11 points, unless the game has been "set." (See Rule 7, Scoring, in the Laws of Badminton, available online at usabadminton.org)

Badminton can be played as a singles or doubles **game.** In singles play, one person must cover the entire court on his/her side of the net. This means that singles play requires more movement and a greater degree of physical conditioning. In doubles play, there are two players on each side; thus there is less court to be covered by each player. This means that strategy and shot making take on a greater role in doubles play. There is also mixed doubles, which means that a doubles team is made up of a man and a woman. Although the strategy and shots used tend to differ somewhat between doubles and mixed doubles, these elements are still considered most important for successful mixed doubles play.

Except for mixed doubles, competition is usually separate for men and women. However, in recreational play, men and women often play against each other. Players of age groups compete, and age is not a barrier to participation. In competition, tournaments are designed to include juniors (under age 21, 18, 16, 14, 12), open division (all ages), and seniors (age 35 years and up in 5-year increments to 80 years and older).

ACTION INVOLVED

A badminton rally always starts with a serve. In singles, a high deep serve is used most of the time. This is usually followed by a combination of clears and drop shots. The object is to move the opponent around the court and create an opening for a smash or another fast shot to win the rally. Many times the rally will be won by a quick clear or drop shot, especially if a combination of shots has forced the opponent out of position. However, it is even more common that the rally ends when a player is forced to make an error (i.e., the shuttle is hit into the net or **out**). With increasing skills, the player should focus on committing fewer errors and increasing the length of each rally. Thus, as players become more skilled, physical conditioning takes on an even greater role. It is not unusual, even on the elite level, for patient players who are in excellent physical condition to play safe shots with the object of committing no errors in the hope that the opponent will instead become impatient and make an error. However, elite players have the skills to force their opponent out of position, to hit clear **winners,** or to play patiently.

out A term used by a player or line judge to indicate the shuttle landed out of court.

In doubles, the short serve is used most of the time. The object is to force the opponents to hit up (where the shuttle can then be contacted above the level of the net), which sets up various types of down shots, such as smashes or drops. The team that can hit down is normally attacking and in control of the rally, and the team that hits up will be on the defensive. Fast drives, half-court shots, and various **net shots** are also common in doubles play. Doubles play is usually faster than singles play because smashes and drives are much more common. Team play and shot selection are extremely important; teams that play well together often are the most successful, even if they are not made up of the most individually skilled players.

winner (also kill, put-away) A smash hit to win the rally.

net shot A shot played to the opponent's forecourt that drops close to the net.

Participants

RULES AND VIOLATIONS

The participants are referred to as players. In singles play, there is one player on each side of the net; in doubles play, there are two players on each side of the net.

The Toss

Before starting play, a coin toss, or racket spin, determines who will serve first. The winner of the toss has the option of serving first, not serving first, or choosing ends; however, only one of these choices can be made. The loser of the toss can then choose one of the remaining alternatives.

Serving

The point (rally) always starts with a serve. An **inning** is the period a player (or team) holds service. The **server** may not start to serve until the opponent is ready, and the opponent is considered ready if an attempt to return the serve is made. To serve or to receive serve, the player must stand within the correct **service court** and may not touch any of the lines with any part of the foot. The player receiving serve cannot move until the shuttle has contacted the server's racket. The shuttle must either land within the correct service court or be played by the opponent in order to count. The shuttle can touch the net and still be in play as long as it lands in the service court or is returned (hit) by the opponent.

inning The period during which a player or team holds the service.
server The player who hits the serve.
service court The singles or doubles court boundary into which the service must be delivered.

fault *A violation of the rules. See Law 13.*

receiver *The player who receives the service.*

The serving motion has to be an underhand motion. The shuttle must not be contacted above waist level, and the racket head must be below the level of the hand and fingers of the racket hand (Figure 2.1). If the server swings and fails to contact the shuttle, it is a **fault**. The service motion must be continuous once it has started, and the server cannot feint or use movements to distract the service **receiver**. In doubles, a player cannot strike a serve intended for his/her partner.

Faults

Faults refer to a violation that will result in a penalty (i.e., the loss of the rally). Here is a list of nine faults:

1. Breaking any of the rules for correct service or service return will result in a fault.
2. If the shuttle lands outside the correct court boundaries (if the shuttle lands on the line, it is considered good), passes under the net, or gets caught in the net, it is a fault. If the shuttle passes outside the net post and flies into the other court, it is not a fault.
3. If the shuttle touches the ceiling, gymnasium walls, a player, or the clothing of a player, it is a fault.
4. If a player touches the net with any part of the racket or his/her body, it is a fault. A player cannot enter the opponent's court with any part of the body, which includes letting momentum carry any body part under the net.
5. A player cannot reach over the net to contact the shuttle, but the racket can follow through over the net after the shuttle has been contacted on the player's side of the net, provided the net is not touched.

Figure 2.1

Racket positions for correct and illegal serves.

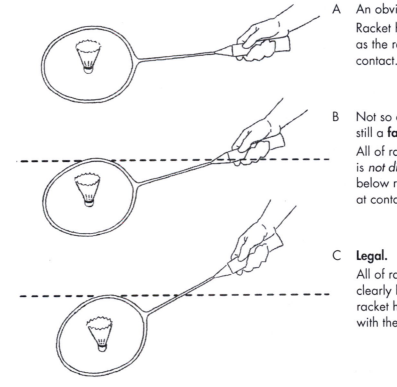

A   An obvious **fault.**
Racket head is as high as the racket hand at contact.

B   Not so obvious—but still a **fault.**
All of racket head is *not discernibly* below racket hand at contact.

C   **Legal.**
All of racket head is clearly below all of racket hand at contact with the shuttle.

Please notice in all cases the shaft of the racket *is pointing down*—yet A and B are faults because the racket head is not *discernibly* below the racket hand upon contact.

6. At the net, a player cannot intentionally hold the racket in a manner so as to block or obstruct the opponent's downward shot. However, putting the racket in front of the face for protection is allowed.

7. A player cannot **double hit** (strike the shuttle twice in succession) before the shuttle is returned to the opponent's court. In doubles, the players on the same side cannot hit successive shots before returning the shuttle, also called a double hit.

8. If a player is hit with the shuttle, regardless of whether the player is standing in or outside the court boundaries, it is a fault.

9. A player may not obstruct his/her opponent in any way.

double hit In singles, one player hitting the shuttle twice in succession, or in doubles, both players hitting the shuttle during the same shot; it is a fault.

Lets

Lets refer to situations where play is stopped for various reasons, but no faults occur and no points are awarded. Instead, the point is replayed. Below are four common reasons for calling a let:

let An incident that requires the replay of a rally. See Rule 14.

1. The serve returner is not ready and lets the serve drop to the floor without attempting a return.

2. A shuttle or player from an adjoining court lands on or steps into the court of play during a point.

3. Sometimes there may be obstructions hanging over the court, such as low beams, lights, ropes, etc. If the shuttle hits any of these obstructions, it may be called a let if the local association has established this as a ground rule. If no such rule is in effect, it would be a fault. If a player intentionally hits a low-hanging obstruction, it is always considered a fault.

4. If the shuttle gets caught in the net but has passed over to the opponent's side, it is a let because the opponent had no fair chance to return it. However, it is a fault on the opponent if he/she hits the net in an attempt to return the shuttle. A shuttle that gets caught in the net but does not go over the net onto the opponent's side is always a fault.

Continuous Play

Play must be continuous during an entire match. A player who does not adhere to this rule may be faulted or disqualified. A player cannot leave the court or receive advice during a match. Furthermore, a player cannot take extra time and rest between points or between games. The only exception is between the second and third games when a 5-minute rest period is allowed if a player requests it. However, this is a local rule (by country) and may not apply in all countries.

FACILITY

The line markings of a badminton court are shown in Figure 2.2. A combination singles and doubles court (the most common markings in school gymnasiums) is 20 feet wide and 44 feet long. Sometimes only the singles court is marked, in which case the court would be 17 feet wide, with the same length. There should be at least 6 feet of clear space between the outer lines of each court and any surrounding courts or walls. However, local conditions do not always allow for such a generous amount of space; in most circumstances, 4 feet of surrounding space is adequate. Sometimes local conditions dictate even less surrounding space, but this makes for less than ideal circumstances. There should be at least 30 feet of unobstructed space above the court. Again, local conditions may dictate less space, and the local organizations will then specify rulings on what constitutes a fault if objects and/or the ceiling is lower than 30 feet above the court.

Figure 2.2

Badminton court diagram with line and court markings.

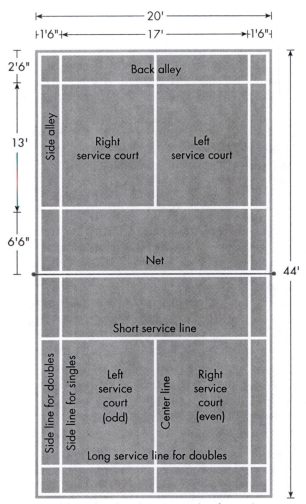

The net divides the court in half. The net posts should be situated on the doubles sidelines, and the net should be hung 5 feet 1 inch above the floor at the post. This will allow for a slight sag of the net toward the middle, but the net height at the center-point of the court should be exactly 5 feet. The lines marking the court are usually white or yellow and should be 1.5 inches wide.

SCORING

love A term used to indicate a score of zero points.

game point A designation to indicate that the rally ends the game if it is won by the server.

A player can score a point only by winning a rally while serving (i.e., winning a rally that started with the opponent serving does not score a point but wins the right to serve). Losing a rally means the player loses either the point or the serve. In men's singles and all doubles matches, a game consists of 15 points; in women's singles, a game consists of 11 points. **Love** indicates zero points. A game does not need to be won by 2 points. **Game point** is the rally that wins (ends) the game; **match point** is the rally that wins (ends) the match. During 15-point games, if the score becomes tied at 14, the first player to reach this score can "set" the game at 3 points, for a total of 17 points. If the player chooses "no set," the game is played to 15 points. Thus, a game will end when the first player reaches 15 points (if no "set") or 17 points (if "set" at 14 points). In women's singles, the game can be "set" at 3 points if the score is tied at 10 points. Thus, women's singles will end when the first player reaches 11 points (no "set") or 13 points if set.

A **match** consists of the best of three games. The players will change ends at the end of each game, as well as after the first player reaches 6 points (in women's singles) or 8 points (in men's singles and all doubles matches). If the players forget to change ends, the change will take place as soon as the mistake is discovered. No points will be replayed.

In singles, the game starts with a serve from the right-hand service court, also called the **even court.** Whenever a player is serving and has an even score, the player will serve from the even court. When the server has an odd point score, the server will serve from the left or **odd court.**

In doubles, the team decides which player will start to serve or receive serve. This will become the "even" player, and he/she will always serve or receive serve in the even court when his/her team's score is even. Similarly, the "odd" player will always serve or receive serve in the odd court when the team's score is odd. The player who is not serving or receiving may stand anywhere on the court during the serve as long as not obstructing the view of the service receiver.

Each doubles team will have two turns at serve (one for each player) before turning the serve over to the other team, except at the start of the game. In doubles, the **first server** serves first, and the **second server** (on the same team) serves next; then the other team serves twice. The team that starts to serve gets only one turn of service and must turn the serve over after a rally is lost. The player who serves must serve from the correct service court. For example, if the team's score is 4 points, the "even" player will serve from the even court. If the serving team wins the point, the "even" player continues to serve, this time from the odd court. If at this point the serving team loses the rally, the "odd" player will serve the second serve from the even court, since the team's score is 5, or odd. If the serving team loses the next rally, the serve goes over to the other team. Since the score is still 5 for the team that lost the serve, the "odd" player will receive serve first, in the even court. When a team wins the serve, the first service will always start from the even court, regardless of the score.

match point A rally that if won by the server ends the match.

setting A method of extending the game when the score is tied near the end of the game. See Rule 7.

match The best two out of three games.

even court The side of the court corresponding with the right service court.

odd court The side of the court corresponding with the left service court.

first server A term in doubles indicating that the player serving is the first server of that inning.

second server A term used in doubles to indicate that the server is the second player to serve in that inning.

ETIQUETTE

As with any sport, it is important to know and act in accordance with a certain etiquette when playing badminton. Since most matches are played without linesmen or referees, players must adhere to accepted rules of conduct. This will make the sport much more enjoyable. Below is a brief list of expected rules of etiquette:

1. Most of the time, players call their own lines (i.e., they make the decision whether a shuttle lands in or out of court on their side of the net). It is extremely important that you make these calls honestly, quickly, and accurately. If the shuttle lands on the line, it is considered good. If you are not sure, you must call it good. If you do not see the shuttle land, you can ask your opponent to make the call. If neither of you sees the shuttle land, you can play a let if both of you agree. However, the more correct call would probably be to consider the shuttle good because you cannot be sure it was out.

2. Call any faults on yourself promptly (touching the net, having the shuttle touch your clothing, etc.).

3. When you are serving, call out the score and make sure your opponent is ready to receive serve.

4. Make sure your serve is legal.

5. If your opponent is serving and the shuttle is on your side of the net at the end of a rally, return the shuttle directly to your opponent.

6. If you tie your opponent at one of the setting points, ask him/her if he/she wishes to "set" the game.

7. Before you start the game, agree with your opponent on which shuttle to use. Ask your opponent first before you change or modify the shuttle once the match has started.

8. Do not slow down the game between points to get extra rest. Remember that play is continuous.

9. During warm-up, hit the shuttle to your opponent so you both get a real chance to warm up.

10. Do not use abusive language or throw your racket.

11. Always play at your best, even if your opponent is not as skilled as you are. Anything less is demeaning.

12. Shake hands and introduce yourself before the match; then also shake hands and thank your opponent following the match.

13. Know the rules well.

14. Learn to win and lose gracefully. Do not blame your defeat on some trivial matter or poor play. Do not belittle your opponent's play if you win. Always compliment the play of your opponent after the match.

Skills and Drills

Executing strokes and mastering shots are the most important skills in the game of badminton. However, these strokes and shots can only be correctly executed if you have the correct racket grip. Therefore, following a discussion of the racket grip and wrist action, this section will focus primarily on how to execute the strokes and will provide various drills that can be used to practice the skills. Although there is no set order for learning most of the strokes, we prefer to start by teaching overhead strokes first, followed by sidearm strokes and then underhand strokes. The service and blocking strokes are variations of one or more of the aforementioned strokes; thus, those strokes will be taught last. Also in this section, footwork and court coverage will be described, along with appropriate drills. A successful player will be able to execute the strokes and cover the court without getting out of position as a result of both correct stroke execution and footwork.

INTRODUCTION

SKILL 1 | Racket Grip

One of the most difficult skills to learn as a beginner is the proper racket grip. In order to be able to execute the strokes appropriately, the player must have the proper grip. If not, a player cannot develop a varied repertoire of shots and hit them with accuracy, power, and **deception.** Consequently, this is the first skill any player should develop. There are three basic grips used in badminton:

1. Forehand grip
2. Backhand grip
3. Frying pan (or hammer) grip

The forehand and backhand grips are obviously used during forehand and backhand shots. The frying pan grip is typically used around the net or for blocking shots. For all grips, it is important to remember the following four points:

1. The grip should be firm but not too tight. If you grip the racket too tightly, it limits racket motion. In the beginning, it is better to grip the racket too loosely instead of too tightly.

deception *Body or racket movement used to lead the receiver to believe the shuttle will be hit at a different speed or direction than it actually is.*

17

2. Think of the racket as an extension of your arm. As you move your arm to execute various shots, it is normal that your grip will vary slightly from shot to shot.

3. There should be space between your index and middle fingers when you grip the racket—do not bunch all your fingers together.

4. The index finger wraps around the racket handle and *does not point up the racket handle toward the shaft*. Pointing the index finger reduces both power and racket mobility.

Forehand Grip

For the forehand grip, think of it in terms of shaking hands with the racket. Open your hand with the fingers slightly separated. As shown in Figure 3.1, place the racket diagonally across the hand, starting across the base of your index finger and ending below the base of the pinkie. The edge of the handle lies over the lifeline of your hand, as shown. The first three fingers are used to grip and control the racket. Wrap your thumb around the racket and rest the ball of the thumb against the middle finger (Figure 3.2). If you look at the racket and hand from the top, a correct grip forms a "V" with the thumb and the index finger over the inside bevel of the racket handle (Figure 3.3). Subtle changes and variations of this grip can now easily be controlled by the thumb and the index finger. During play, the grip will vary slightly by changing the pressure points and by sliding the hand up and down the handle. Holding the racket near the butt of the handle helps to increase power, whereas choking up on the handle will provide more control. Consequently, choking up is often useful for serving and net play.

Figure 3.1 (on left)

Let the racket handle rest diagonally across the fingers before gripping it.

Figure 3.2 (on right)

Side view of forehand grip. Note position of the thumb, index finger, and three holding fingers.

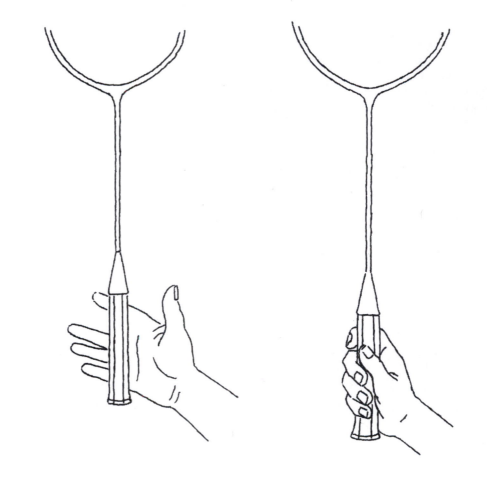

Backhand Grip

Although the basic forehand grip can be used to hit the overhead backhand shots, most players use a slight variation that seems to be more effective. From the forehand grip, move the thumb up to the left bevel of the racket handle, as shown in Figure 3.4. The inside of the thumb should now exert pressure on the bevel of the racket handle. This grip is most effective for overhead shots, such as clears, smashes, and drops.

A variation of the above grip is the thumbs-up backhand grip. For this grip, the thumb is moved straight up the flat back of the racket, pointing toward the racket head (Figure 3.5); the thumb should be closer to the racket head than the index finger. This grip is best used for low drives and blocks, particularly for shots close to the body. This grip is also used for delicate shots at the net, but the racket is gripped more loosely and the hand should be choked up to provide better control.

Frying Pan Grip

The **frying pan grip,** a variation of the forehand grip, is used primarily for net play when the shuttle is above the level of the net and can be hit down. The racket is turned a quarter-turn compared with the normal forehand grip, and the thumb is placed at the side of the racket handle (Figure 3.6). In other words, you grab the racket handle as if you were grabbing a frying pan. A common mistake among beginners is to use this grip for all forehand shots because it is easier to hit the shuttle cleanly. However, the frying pan grip does not allow for the same deception and control as the standard grip for most forehand shots and should not be used away from the net.

Figure 3.3
Top view of forehand grip. Note "V" (between index finger and thumb) positioned over inside bevel of the racket handle.

frying pan grip A variation of the forehand grip, used primarily for net play when the shuttle is above the level of the net.

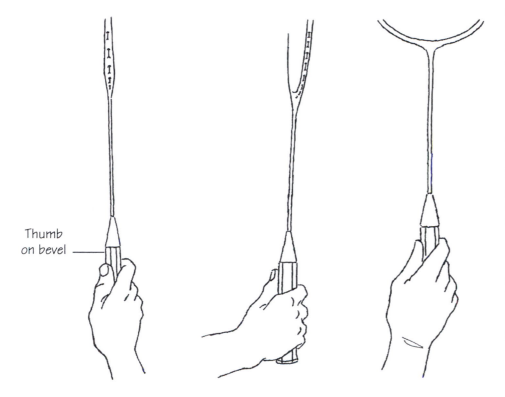

Thumb
on bevel

Figure 3.4 (on left)
Standard backhand grip with thumb placement on inside bevel of grip.

Figure 3.5 (center)
Thumbs-up backhand grip. Note the thumb is closer to the racket shaft than the index finger.

Figure 3.6 (on right)
Frying pan (or hammer) grip.

SKILL 2 | Wrist (Cocking and Uncocking of the Wrist) and Forearm Action

backswing The initial part of a stroke in which the racket is taken back and the wrist cocked.

Execution of the basic forehand and backhand shots requires a combination of wrist and forearm movement that we will describe as wrist action. The wrist moves from a fully extended position to a hyperextended position during the **backswing** and from the hyperextended position to full extension during the movements that accelerate the racket to hit the shuttle. In badminton, there is no significant flexion of the wrist from the fully extended position to the flexed position or from the flexed position to extension (Figure 3.7a). In addition, the wrist flexes from side to side. Wrist movement toward the thumb is called radial flexion and movement back toward the fifth finger is ulnar flexion (Figure 3.7b). Accompanying these wrist movements are inward (pronation) and outward (supination) rotation of the forearm (Figure 3.8).

Figure 3.7

Wrist action. (a) Wrist extension and hyperextension are important movements in the badminton shot. Wrist flexion should be avoided. (b) Radial and ulnar flexion provide important racket mobility during the cocking and uncocking phases of the badminton stroke.

Figure 3.8

The forearm movements of pronation and supination provide power for most badminton shots.

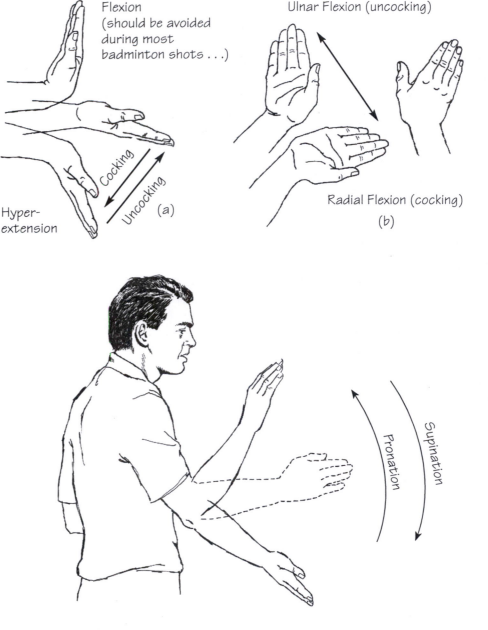

Cocking will be the term used to describe the wrist and forearm movements occurring during the backswing. Uncocking will be the term that describes wrist and forearm movement during the forward swing, which accelerates the racket head through contact with the shuttle.

During the forehand stroke backswing, cocking includes hyperextension and radial flexion of the wrist (Figure 3.9) and supination of the forearm. Uncocking involves extension and ulnar flexion of the wrist and pronation of the forearm.

For the backhand stroke backswing, cocking includes hyperextension and radial flexion of the wrist and pronation of the forearm. Uncocking involves extension and ulnar flexion of the wrist and supination of the forearm. These wrist action movements are outlined in Table 3.1.

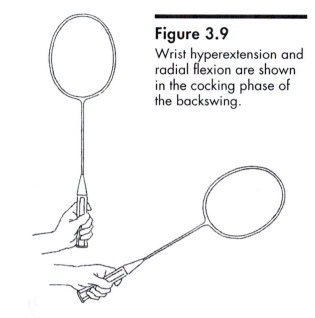

Figure 3.9
Wrist hyperextension and radial flexion are shown in the cocking phase of the backswing.

TABLE 3.1	Wrist action and forearm movements.		
STROKE	**MOVEMENT**	**JOINT**	**ACTION**
Forehand	Cocking	Wrist	Hyperextension, radial flexion
	(backswing)	Forearm	Supination (outward rotation)
Forehand	Uncocking	Wrist	Extension, ulnar flexion
	(forward swing)	Forearm	Pronation (inward rotation)
Backhand	Cocking	Wrist	Hyperextension, radial flexion
	(backswing)	Forearm	Pronation
Backhand	Uncocking	Wrist	Extension, ulnar flexion
	(forward swing)	Forearm	Supination

SKILL 3 Overhead Stroke: Forehand Shots

There are three basic overhead forehand shots: (1) clears, or **lobs,** (2) smashes, and (3) drops. These shots can all have several variations, including around-the-head shots (which will be explained later). The important premise for the overhead forehand shots is that you want to make all shots look the same so your opponent cannot tell what shot will be hit when you hit the shuttle. Thus, the basic techniques for all these shots are the same; the only variations are the contact point, the speed and power at impact, and the **follow-through.** Most of the time these shots are hit from the backcourt, usually between the long doubles service line and the back boundary line. The complete stroke consists of a preparation phase, a backswing, a swing (acceleration to contact), and a follow-through. The basic mechanics that should be followed for all these shots are listed in six steps:

1. Grip the racket with a relaxed but firm forehand grip.
2. Wait for the shuttle in the ready position. Stand with your feet shoulder-width apart and parallel to the net. Hold the racket chest high in a relaxed position in

lob (also clear) A shot hit high and deep to the opponent's backcourt.

follow-through Movement of the racket and the player's body after racket–shuttle contact during the execution of a shot.

Figure 3.10

Standard **ready position** with legs spread about shoulder-width apart and racket head up and in front of the body.

Head up ←

Leaning eagerly in anticipation of shot ←

Knees bent ←

Weight on the balls of the feet ←

Ready position A position to which players try to return after each shot

front of the body with the racket head up (Figure 3.10). This position will allow you to move easily to position yourself under the shuttle as it is hit toward you.

3. In the preparation phase, turn your non-racket shoulder toward the net and extend the racket elbow away from your body at shoulder height (Figure 3.11a). Your shoulders should now be in line and perpendicular to the net. Lift your non-racket leg up in the air, and slightly flex the racket-side knee.

4. For the backswing, start by cocking (hyperextending) your wrist and rotating (supinating) your forearm outward while reaching backward (Figure 3.11b).

5. For the swing, as your hips and shoulders rotate to a parallel position with the net, extend the forearm, followed by rotation (pronation) of your elbow toward the net, with the wrist still in a cocked position (Figure 3.11c). Your body weight is shifted forward, and the non-racket leg will move downward. Just before the racket contacts the shuttle, the wrist is uncocked to bring the racket flush to the shuttle at contact (Figure 3.11d). Your body may be airborne through the contact point, and you should land on your non-racket leg at the beginning of the follow-through.

6. In the follow-through, let the racket rotate down in front of your body. Allow your forearm to complete the rotation and the wrist to become fully extended while keeping your elbow at shoulder height (Figure 3.11e–f). Step forward with the racket-side leg as you lower your arm. Return to the ready position using a small hop (Figure 3.11g).

CUES: 1. Reach way back in the backswing.

2. Turn your non-racket shoulder toward the net during the preparation phase.

3. Think of the shoulder rotation during the swing as uncoiling the body (i.e., the motion starts with the hips followed by the shoulders, like a coil springing back to its original position).

4. Reach for the shuttle and try to contact it as high as possible.

Figure 3.11

Important phases of the overhead forehand stroke: (a) ready position,
(b) backswing, (c) swing phase, (d) contact, and (e–f) follow-through.

(a)   (b)   (c)   (d)

(e)   (f)   (g)

TABLE 3.2	Common swing problems.	
COMMON PROBLEM	**RESULT**	**CORRECTION**
Frying pan grip	No forearm rotation Poor power Poor deception	Use a standard forehand grip.
Poor forearm rotation	Poor timing Slicing the shuttle Poor power Hitting the shuttle to the left of the target	Adjust rotation to allow your forearm to rotate 90° prior to contact. Continue rotation during the follow-through. Shuttle contact should be flush. Racket grip may be too tight; loosen your grip.
"Poking" at the shuttle instead of swinging hard	Poor power and distance	Use a full backswing. Swing hard. Hit through the shuttle.
Uncocking the wrist before contact	Poor power and distance Poor deception	Loosen racket grip. Use a half swing (no follow-through) to learn to feel your wrist pushing the shuttle; then add a full swing.
Poor hip and shoulder rotation	Poor power and distance	Uncoil your upper body—rotate your hips and shoulders hard. Shift your weight from the racket to the non-racket foot. Use a small hop when transferring your weight.
Low point of contact	Poor distance Poor deception	Keep your elbow up during the swing. Reach for the shuttle.

5. Snap the racket into the shuttle at contact (i.e., rotate your forearm and flex your wrist as quickly as possible).
6. Bring the racket head back up in front of your body where it is in sight as you return to the ready position.

Table 3.2 lists some common swing problems and their results, as well as corrections for the problems.

Drills for Overhead Forehand Shots

Drill #1: Stroke Practice

This drill is meant to let you practice each phase of the stroke without actually hitting a shuttle. Instead, the focus should be on producing the appropriate stroke mechanics.

1. Start in the ready position, feet parallel to the net, racket up, and knees slightly bent.
2. Turn the shoulders and raise the racket to the ready position. Hold this position for 2 seconds.
3. Start the backswing and cock wrist, but do this very slowly (almost in slow motion). Make sure the racket is way back, with the **shaft** perpendicular to the net. Pause for 1 or 2 seconds before proceeding.

shaft *The part of the racket connecting the handle and the head.*

4. Slowly, again almost in slow motion, start the swing. Lift your non-racket side leg, start the hip and shoulder rotation, and then start the arm motion. Focus on keeping your elbow up, completely extending the arm and reaching as high as possible. Watch your forearm rotate and the wrist become uncocked as you imagine contact with the shuttle. Make sure that you transfer the weight from the racket to the non-racket side leg at contact. Pause for 1 or 2 seconds to check for elbow height, forearm rotation, and wrist flexion.

5. Complete the follow-through, and step forward with the right foot until you return to the ready position.

6. Repeat steps 1 through 5 several times until the stroke feels comfortable.

CUE: Try to emulate the drawings in Figure 3.11 during each of the different phases of the stroke. It might also help working with a partner who can tell you if you are doing something wrong.

Drill #2: Continued Stroke Practice

As you become more comfortable with the stroke, conduct the same drill but without a pause in the stroke, except between the ready position and the preparation phase. Most players will hold the preparation phase for a short time as they wait for the shuttle. As you become better, use a small hop to transfer from the ready phase to the preparation phase, and use another small hop to become airborne when you transfer your weight during the swing phase. Concentrate on the same points, trying to perfect the stroke motion.

Drill #3: Add Movement

Start in the middle of the court, then move backward for two steps before initiating the stroke. Concentrate on completing the stroke in one smooth motion at the completion of your movement. Return to the middle of the court at the completion of your follow-through; then start over.

CUE: As with drill #1, it helps if you try to emulate the positions shown in Figure 3.11. Work with a partner who can give you feedback on what you are doing right or wrong.

Drill #4: Add a Shuttle

Have a partner stand on the other side of the court, facing you. Your partner will then hit a shuttle to you, and you will execute the stroke and hit the shuttle over the net. See Figure 3.12 for approximate placement of yourself and your partner. At this point, it is most important to think about executing the stroke appropriately; do not worry about where you hit the shuttle.

1. Start with a slow swing, concentrating on executing a full backswing and the correct mechanics of the swing. The shuttle will not be hit very far, but do not worry about that.

2. Have your partner observe your stroke and give you hints (i.e., Was your backswing complete? Did you turn your shoulders? Did you reach up for the shuttle? Did you transfer your weight?).

3. As you become more comfortable, speed up the swing and concentrate on hitting the shuttle harder. Aim to hit it high and deep.

Figure 3.12
Drill positions for learning overhead forehand shots. Server hits clear into hitting zone for receiver to practice clears.

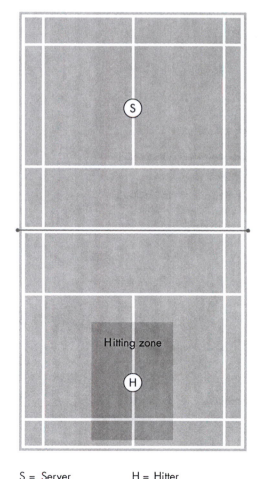

S = Server   H = Hitter

Figure 3.13

Overhead stroke contact angles for (a) defensive clears and (b) offensive clears.

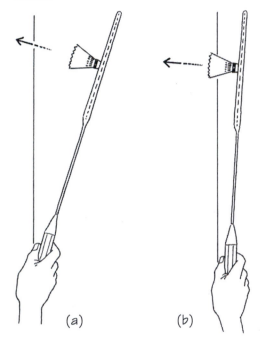

(a)   (b)

4. You should hear a pop as the shuttle hits the racket—this indicates a solid hit. If you hear more of a swish sound, you are slicing the shuttle.

5. Complete six to eight clean hits with a good pop sound, then switch court positions with your partner and help him/her. You can learn a substantial amount from watching and helping each other.

CUE: *Do not worry about where you hit the shuttle at this point. You should concentrate on having good swing mechanics and making solid contact with the shuttle.*

Overhead Forehand Clear

There are two types of clear (or lob) shots: defensive clears and offensive clears. Both types of clears are hit high, with the shuttle landing near your opponent's back boundary line. The defensive clear is hit at a substantial upward **trajectory.** This is achieved by the racket angle at contact. Figure 3.13 shows the contact angle and Figure 3.14 shows the expected trajectory of both types of clears.

The defensive clear is used to allow you time to get back to a good receiving position near the center of the court and to make your opponent move as much as possible. Thus, besides being a defensive shot that helps you get out of trouble, it is often used to fatigue an opponent, especially if you know that you are in better physical condition. However, you should not expect to use this shot as a point-getter.

The offensive clear (also called an **attacking clear**) is hit with a flatter trajectory, but still high enough to just go over your opponent's racket and land near the back boundary line (see Figure 3.14). This shot is used to get the shuttle behind your opponent, thus making it as difficult as possible for him/her to return the shuttle. This shot is often used as a point-getter or as a **setup** for a winner. The flatter trajectory is achieved both by

Figure 3.14

Overhead stroke trajectories for (a) defensive clears and (b) offensive clears.

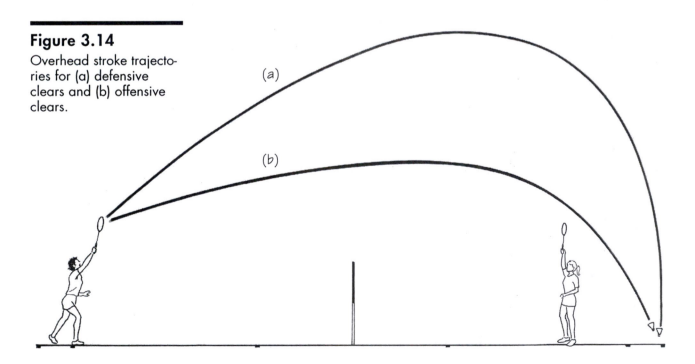

(a)

(b)

the angle of contact and by contacting the shuttle more in front of the body (see Figure 3.13). Both types of clears are hit very forcefully, with almost full power, for the shuttle to go all the way to your opponent's back boundary line.

Drill #5: Defensive Clears

1. With a partner, start at opposite sides of the net. The setter will be at midcourt depth, and the hitter will start near the back boundary line (see Figure 3.15 for clarification).
2. The hitter will practice the defensive clear by using the overhead forehand stroke, concentrating on hitting the shuttle high and deep. Since it often takes some practice before you can hit the shuttle from end line to end line, it helps if the setter stands near midcourt (see Figure 3.15a).
3. Your partner will return the shuttle, also using a defensive clear.
4. As you get better and develop more power, gradually have your setter move back so eventually both of you are hitting the shot close to the back boundary line.
5. When both of you can comfortably perform the shot, include more movement by returning to a center court base position between each shot (see Figure 3.15b).

Drill #6: Offensive Clears

Since the defensive clear is a more basic shot than the offensive clear, do not try the offensive clear until you have mastered the defensive clear.

1. Work in groups of three. Figure 3.16 shows how you will be placed at the start of the drill. Player A will be the hitter (i.e., the person who will be performing the offensive clear), player B will serve as an obstruction, and player C will be the setter.

trajectory The flight pattern of the shuttle.
attacking clear (offensive clear) A low, flat clear used to run the opponent to the backcourt.
setup A shot that gives the opponent an easy chance to win the rally.

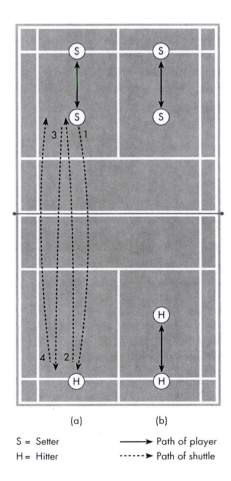
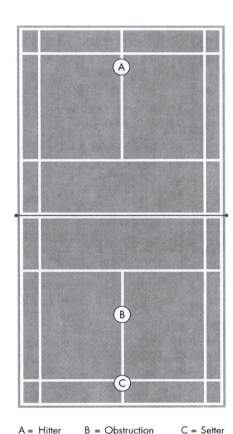

(a) (b)

S = Setter   → Path of player
H = Hitter   ----→ Path of shuttle

A = Hitter   B = Obstruction   C = Setter

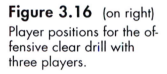

Figure 3.15 (on left) Defensive clear drill: (a) Basic stroking positions and (b) drill with added movement.

Figure 3.16 (on right) Player positions for the offensive clear drill with three players.

Figure 3.17

Side view of attacking clear drill to show shuttle flight pattern.

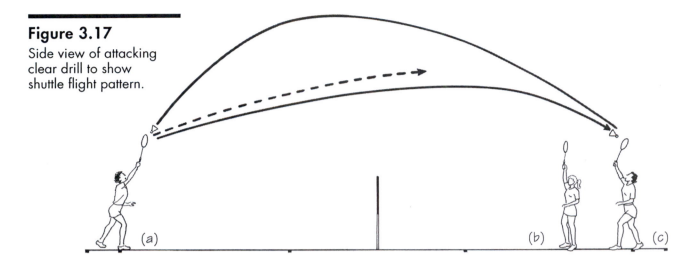

2. Player A will hit offensive clears, trying to hit the shuttle just over player B's racket to player C (Figure 3.17). Player C will return the shuttle using a high defensive clear. Player B will stand at midcourt, with the racket extended up in the air, as an obstruction.

3. After 10 to 15 shots, switch positions; do this until all players have practiced the offensive clear.

4. As you become better, have player B try to cut off your shot (without moving backward). Player A should focus on hitting the shuttle over player B's racket but still land the shuttle inbounds.

5. Hit to the corners.

CUES: 1. *Power on both types of clears comes from correct stroke mechanics and footwork. Thus, focus on positioning your body underneath the shuttle in the preparation position before initiating the shot. Focus on correct stroke mechanics. Review Figure 3.11.*

2. *Use a full backswing and swing hard, snapping the racket head into the shuttle.*

Table 3.3 lists some common clear problems and their results, as well as corrections for the problems.

TABLE 3.3 Common clear problems.		
COMMON PROBLEM	**RESULT**	**CORRECTION**
Trajectory too high	Poor distance	Adjust the point of contact—you are probably contacting the shuttle behind your head. The contact point should be over your racket shoulder.
Trajectory too low	Poor distance (you will not be able to hit the shuttle over your opponent's racket to make him/her move)	Adjust the point of contact—you are probably contacting the shuttle too far in front of your body or your racket angle is closed. Reach for the shuttle—your point of contact may also be low.
Trajectory OK but power poor	Poor distance (shuttle will not go over your opponent's racket to make him/her move)	Focus on your swing—make sure that your swing mechanics are correct. The most common mistake is using a short backswing and poking at the shuttle. Swing hard and snap the racket into the shuttle at contact.

Overhead Forehand Smash

The smash is the primary attacking shot and is most often used as a point-getter. It is hit with maximal, or near maximal, velocity and power and with a steep downward angle. Figure 3.18 shows the contact angle and Figure 3.19 depicts the trajectories of the smash. The flat smash can be hit with more power than the steep smash, (i.e., the steeper the angle, the less velocity you achieve). However, flat smashes are easier for your opponent to return than steep smashes. Both types of smashes are executed using the basic overhead forehand stroke but with more racket velocity, and the contact point is more in front of the body than when hitting the clear.

Drill #7: Forehand Smashes

1. With a partner, start in the same position as for the defensive clear (Figure 3.15a). Your partner will hit a high defensive clear to you from his/her midcourt position, aiming for the long service line for doubles.
2. Execute the shot, either the steep or flat smash. Your partner should let the shuttle drop so you can see where it lands.
3. After 10 to 15 shots, or when you are comfortable, allow your partner to try to return your smash. This will let you know how well you are executing the shot. After your partner returns the smash (or not, if you hit a winner), stop and start again.
4. Switch court positions so both players hit and return smash shots.
5. As you become more comfortable, try to aim for the sideline. A smash hit close to the sideline is very difficult to return.

CUES:
1. Use a standard forehand grip, and concentrate on your forearm rotation. Many beginning players will change their grip to a frying pan grip when hitting the smash. However, this will not allow you to hit a good steep smash, nor will your shot be deceptive.
2. Focus on reaching for the shuttle and contact it in front of your body. It is common to drop the arm at contact in an attempt to pull the shuttle downward. This does not work and will not allow you to achieve a good angle on the smash.
3. Keep your elbow up in the follow-through (see Figure 3.11e–f). This will help to complete the forearm rotation and increase the chances of the shuttle going over the net.

Table 3.4 lists some common smash problems and their causes, as well as corrections for the problems.

Figure 3.18
Racket–shuttle contact for the smash shot.

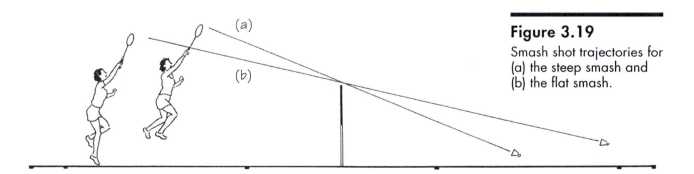

Figure 3.19
Smash shot trajectories for (a) the steep smash and (b) the flat smash.

TABLE 3.4	Common smash problems.	
COMMON PROBLEM	**CAUSE**	**CORRECTION**
Most shots hit into the net	Racket angle too steep Low contact point Shuttle contacted too far in front of body	Adjust the racket angle—hit the shot a little more flat. Reach for the shuttle and contact the shuttle as high as possible. Contact the shuttle about 1 foot in front of your body. Keep your elbow up in follow through.
Poor power—most shots sliced	Not enough forearm rotation Poor shoulder rotation	Rotate your forearm completely and vigorously—snap your forearm into the shuttle. Uncoil your upper body and rotate the shoulders toward the shuttle.
Shot trajectory too flat (shuttle lands close to back boundary line or out-of-bounds)	Poor angle of contact Low contact point Frying pan grip	Contact the shuttle a little more in front of your body. Adjust the racket angle downward. Reach for the shuttle and make contact as high as possible. Check your grip—make sure you have a correct forehand grip.

Figure 3.20

Racket–shuttle contact
angles for (a) the loop drop
and (b) the attacking drop.

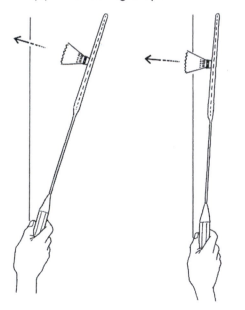

cross-court A shot hit
diagonally from one side
of the court to the other.

face The strung surface
of the racket.

Overhead Forehand Drop

There are two types of overhead forehand drop shots: the slow or loop drop and the attacking or fast drop shot. The angle of contact and basic trajectories of both drops are shown in Figure 3.20. Drop shots are used to force your opponent out of position and to make him/her run longer distances during a rally. The combination of drop shots and clears can be used effectively either to move your opponent out of position and set up a smash or to tire out your opponent.

The slow or loop drop is easier to learn and execute. You perform this shot by slowing down your swing just before contact and executing a short follow-through. The contact point should be in a similar position to the defensive clear. Thus, think about this shot as if you were executing a defensive clear, but use a lot less force and power just before you hit the shuttle. You want to hit this shot so the shuttle drops as close to the net as possible.

The attacking drop is hit faster, with a flatter trajectory (Figure 3.21), and can often be executed for a winner if your opponent is out of position. This shot is often referred to as a controlled smash but is executed with much less velocity. This shot can be made to look exactly like a smash or a clear if executed by slicing or cutting the shuttle. Using this technique, the racket head has a lot of velocity, but the contact of the shuttle and racket face is not flush, thus reducing shuttle speed. This slicing motion can be accomplished in two ways:

1. *Slice.* To hit a **cross-court** drop from the even court or a straight drop from the odd court, you will slice the shuttle by swinging at about a 45° angle with the net and strike the shuttle without rotating your forearm, similarly to what is done in a tennis serve. During the end of the swing phase of your stroke, just before contact, slow down the forearm rotation so you contact the shuttle before the **face** of your racket head is flush with the shuttle. The rest of the stroke is exactly the

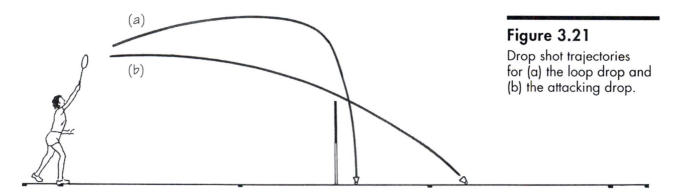

Figure 3.21

Drop shot trajectories for (a) the loop drop and (b) the attacking drop.

same as previously described. This shot is called a **slice**, a **cut shot**, or an **off-speed shot**.

2. *Reverse cut.* To hit a cross-court drop from the odd court or a straight drop from the even court, you need to overrotate your forearm before contact. In other words, the forearm rotation should be beyond flush, as if you have already started your follow-through when you actually contact the shuttle. The contact point is slightly to the left of the slow drop contact point. You are now slicing to guide the shuttle in the opposite direction compared with the drop from the even court. The slice motion hit from right to left is called the reverse cut drop shot (see Figure 3.22).

The slice and reverse cut drops are very easy to learn for some beginning players and very difficult for others. Even some very accomplished players do not use all variations of these drop shots.

slice (cut shot, off-speed shot) A shot in which the racket brushes across the shuttle at an angle to the direction of the swing in order to reduce shuttle speed and change the direction of the shuttle flight.

Drill #8: Slow Drops

Since the loop drop is easier to hit, attempt this drop before attempting the attacking drop shots.

1. Work with a partner. Your partner will stand on the opposite court, close to the net, and hit high defensive clears to you (Figure 3.23). Your starting position should be in the backcourt over the long doubles service line.
2. Hit a slow drop off each defensive clear. Focus on executing a complete and correct stroke, but slow it down to decrease the shuttle speed.
3. Your partner should let your drops fall to the floor so you can see where they land. This will let you know when your shots are hit in the right spot.
4. After 12 to 15 shots, switch court positions with your partner.
5. As you become comfortable with this shot, try drops from all positions along the back boundary line. Start with hitting only straight drop shots; then try to hit some cross-court shots. Your partner should still let the shuttle hit the floor to let you evaluate the success of your shots.
6. After 15 to 20 shots, switch court positions with your partner.

CUES: 1. Focus on reaching for the shuttle, and make contact at the highest possible point. Beginning players often drop their elbow and execute the shot with a bent arm.

Figure 3.22

Execution of the drop shot with a reverse cut motion.

Figure 3.23

Drop shot drill patterns for (a) straight-ahead drops, (b) cross-court reverse cut drops, and (c) cross-court slice shots.

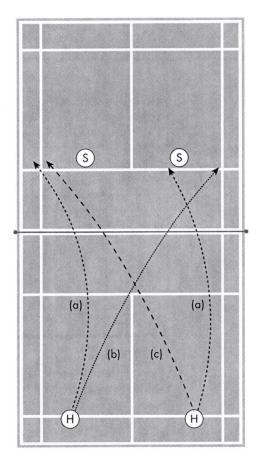

S = Server   H = Hitter

2. Do not cut back on your backswing. Execute a complete backswing, but slow down the swing just before contact.

3. Do not eliminate the follow-through. You don't want to poke at the shuttle; you want to execute a complete stroke and actually hit it, but softer than during a smash or clear.

4. Keeping the wrist stable at contact will reduce power and provide deception when executing the slow drop shot.

Drill #9: Attacking Drops

The attacking drop is easier to learn, starting with the cross-court drop. Start in the even (right court); hit each drop cross-court aiming for the short, outside corner of your opponent's **short service line** (see Figure 3.23).

1. Work with a partner. Your partner will stand in the opposite odd court, close to the net and hit high defensive clears cross-court to you. Your starting position should be on the even side of the court and near the long doubles service line.

2. From your position, hit a fast drop cross-court (Figure 3.23c). Focus on reaching for the shuttle and cutting it as you make contact. Do not worry about hitting it in the court in the beginning. It is more important to get the feel of executing good racket speed and cutting (slicing) the shuttle. As you get more comfortable, increase the racket speed.

3. Your partner should let each shot drop to the floor so you can see where it lands.

4. Complete 12 to 15 shots and switch court positions with your partner.

5. When you become better and can hit most of your shots in the court, try to vary the speed on the drop. An attacking drop shot can be hit with different speeds to further confuse your opponent.

6. Switch from the even to the odd court, and hit the drop shot to the backhand side of your opponent (see Figure 3.23b). For this shot, focus on overrotating, almost as if you are making contact during your follow-through. Use the same drill as described in the even court.

Drill #10: Straight-Ahead Drop Shots

Executing the attacking drop shot as a straight-ahead drop is more difficult than hitting cross-court. For a straight drop, you have less room to the sideline, thus less room for error. In the odd court, you can compensate by turning your body slightly toward the **center line** of the court during your preparation. This will also make it look as if you are hitting a cross-court drop and thus increases your deception. You should also come over the top of the shuttle more than usual. This type of shot is usually only performed by more advanced players because of its difficulty. Practice the shot by using the same two drills described above; then practice this shot from both the even and the odd court (see Figure 3.23a).

short service line The forecourt boundary line over which the service must pass.

center line The line that divides the left and right service courts.

CUES: 1. As for the loop drop shot, do not drop your elbow, and make sure you reach for the shuttle.

TABLE 3.5	Common problems of the overhead drop shot.	
COMMON PROBLEM	**CAUSE**	**CORRECTION**
Shots hit mostly into the net	Low contact point Swing too slow Racket angle at contact closed Poor follow-through Too much slice	Reach for the shuttle at contact. Speed up the swing and contact the shuttle a little harder. Open the racket angle at contact. Follow through appropriately. Contact the shuttle more solidly, with less slice.
Shots hit with upward arc	Racket angle too open at contact Contact point too far over or behind head	Close the racket angle at contact. Contact the shuttle about 1 foot in front of your body.
Shots land too far into opponent's court	Swing too forceful Racket angle at contact too open	Slow down the swing. Close the angle at contact.

2. The key to effectiveness of the attacking drop is how well you execute the slice of the drop shot. Experiment by trying to slice the shot with different speed and racket motion until you get a feel for how you can consistently hit this shot.
3. Make sure you execute the weight shift, including the body turn. Do not try to hit the shot using arm motion only.

Table 3.5 lists some common problems of the overhead drop shot, as well as their causes and possible corrections.

SKILL 4 The Around-the-Head "Shot"

The **around-the-head shot** is actually not a shot but a stroke, since clears, smashes, and drops can be hit with this modified forehand stroke, giving the advantage of providing forehand power on the backhand side. This stroke is used to cover the backhand side of the court but has the disadvantage of requiring greater body movement to reach the shuttle. The stroke also makes the body fall backwards away from the net after it is executed, thus requiring more movement to recover between shots. Therefore, it is often suggested that this stroke only be used at three-quarter court, not all the way over to the backhand side. The basic mechanics, shown in Figure 3.24, include these six steps:

1. Use a standard forehand grip.
2. From the ready position, move backward and jump (slightly) off the racket-side foot. If right-handed, you will be rotating to the left and land on the left leg, but deeper in the court.
3. As you move to the shuttle, flex the upper body to the left, and extend the upper arm over the head.
4. With as much backswing as your position allows without dropping the racket head down, start the swing. Rotate your forearm and uncock the wrist as usual.

around-the-head shot
A stroke hit from the backhand side of the body with a forehand stroking pattern.

Figure 3.24

Around-the-head stroking pattern.

5. Keep your forearm above the head through the follow-through until the racket is extended in front of you.

6. During the follow-through, you will land on the non-racket side leg and immediately push off toward the base position.

Drill #11: Around-the-Head Shots

Use the same drills as discussed above for each shot, depending on whether you are practicing clears, smashes, or drop shots. Make sure you start the drill with swing mechanics, since this is a slightly different swing motion than for the regular forehand stroke.

1. Work on getting the footwork correct. Move two steps back, execute the jump and the swing, then return to midcourt.

2. Execute the defensive and offensive clear drills using the around-the-head shot. The setter must make sure that the shuttle is hit to the backhand side of the receiver.

3. Execute the loop drop shot drill, using the around-the-head shot. The attacking drop shot can be executed properly only with a straight drop and cross-court drop from the odd court, so practice only those attacking drop shots.

4. Execute the smash drills using the around-the-head shot.

CUES:
1. Extend your racket elbow as high as possible, and focus on trying to reach with your hand as far to the left as possible. This will extend your reach.

2. Make sure you have a good backswing. Many players cut back on the backswing when they learn the around-the-head shot, but this will limit your power and make it difficult to clear or smash.

3. Make sure you complete the follow-through with your racket arm above your head. Since you will often be somewhat out of position after executing an around-the-head shot, the backswing and follow-through are even more important to ensure that you generate power from this shot.

TABLE 3.6 Common problems of the around-the-head shot.		
COMMON PROBLEM	**CAUSE**	**CORRECTION**
Falling back more than one step when executing the shot	Jumping off the non-racket instead of the racket side leg. Leaning back too far	Jump off your racket side leg. Work harder to position your body behind the shuttle.
Poor power on clears and smashes	Poor backswing Poor flexibility, limiting the reach behind your head (leads to a poor backswing) Contact too far behind your head Poor forearm rotation	Reach farther back and make sure you have a complete backswing. Work on increasing the flexibility of your shoulder and upper arm. Contact the shuttle right over your non-racket shoulder or slightly in front of your head. Rotate your forearm.

4. Make sure that you can execute the hop correctly and land on your non-racket side leg. Your non-racket side leg should act as a stopper to prevent you from falling farther back into the court. It should also be able to generate enough force to propel you forward so that you can get back into position for the next shot.

Table 3.6 lists some common problems of the around-the-head shot, as well as their causes and possible corrections.

Other common problems of the around-the-head shots are the same as for the standard overhead shots described above.

SKILL 5 Overhead Stroke: Intermediate and Advanced Forehand Shots

Once you have mastered the basic shots just discussed, the major difference between a beginner, intermediate, and advanced player is the speed, accuracy, and amount of deception of the shot. Advanced players hit faster shots with more accuracy, and they make virtually every shot look the same. This makes it almost impossible to detect whether he/she is hitting a clear, a drop, or a smash until the shuttle has been struck. Furthermore, an advanced player can execute straight-ahead or cross-court shots with virtually identical swings. Finally, most advanced players have very good footwork, enhancing their ability to get into position to execute each shot. Thus, once you have mastered the basic shots, work on further developing your skills in this order.

1. *Try to hit all your shots with virtually the same motion.* Racket preparation, the backswing, and the swing phase should look almost identical for all shots. Control of which shot you decide to hit will depend on the contact point of the shuttle, the amount of forearm rotation and wrist action used in the shot, and the speed of the follow-through. Use the same drills as previously described, but focus on hitting all shots from the same motion.

2. *Increase the speed of your shots.* Advanced players hit quicker, stronger shots, even for drop shots. Use the same drills as described earlier for each shot, but try to hit them a little quicker, using the same motion on all shots. For the

clears, this usually means hitting more offensive clears with a lower trajectory. For the drop shots, it means cutting or slicing the shuttle more at contact.

3. *Work on accuracy.* Practice enough so that you can hit each shot to within 1 foot of where you are aiming. This will take practice and repetition.

4. *Work on developing proper footwork.* This means executing your shots off the correct foot and being able to perform the small jumps involved in each shot. However, you also need to work on proper footwork for court coverage. See the section on Footwork for the discussion on this.

SKILL 6 | Overhead Stroke: Backhand Shots

As with the forehand, there are three basic overhead backhand shots: (1) clears, (2) smashes, and (3) drops. These shots can also have several variations. The important premise for the overhead backhand stroke is that you want to make all shots look the same so your opponent cannot tell what you will do when you hit the shuttle. Thus, the basic techniques for all these shots are the same; the only variations are the contact point, the speed and power at impact, and the follow-through, just as for the overhead forehand shots. Most of the time these shots are hit from the backcourt, often between the doubles service line and the back boundary line. The basic mechanics for all these shots are listed in six steps:

1. Grip the racket with a relaxed but firm regular backhand grip. Avoid the thumbs-up grip for the overhead backhand shots.
2. You will wait for the shuttle in the ready position, just as for the forehand shots.
3. In the preparation phase, as you position yourself under the shuttle, your back should face the net. Step with your racket-side leg toward the back boundary line, with your back still facing the net (Figure 3.25). The timing of this can be tricky because the racket-side foot should make contact with the floor about the same time as the shuttle is contacted. Keep the racket head up in front of your body (see Figure 3.25).

Figure 3.25

Overhead backhand stroking pattern.

4. For the backswing, bring your elbow up to shoulder level in front of the body. Cock the wrist by hyperextending your wrist and rotate (pronate) your forearm inward at the same time (see Figure 3.25).

5. For the swing, bring your elbow up and out toward the point of contact (see Figure 3.25). Extend your arm, bringing the racket head up above the head. Rotate your forearm outward (supinate), and flex your wrist to full extension (see Figure 3.25). Notice that the arm is extended outward and up, and the shuttle is contacted to the side of the body, not over your head or your shoulder. Contact should be made as high as possible but with a slight bend at the elbow, which allows you to generate more power from outward rotation of the upper arm.

6. The follow-through is very short. It consists primarily of the hyperextension of the wrist and the completion of the forearm rotation. The follow-through should be completed with your racket arm directed toward the racket-side sideline and the racket shaft pointed toward the net (see Figure 3.25).

CUES: 1. Keep your elbow up at shoulder height during the backswing.

2. Make sure your back is pointed toward the net throughout the stroke.

3. Work on coordinating the snap by timing your elbow extension, forearm rotation, and wrist snap.

4. Turn to your right after completion of the stroke to get back into position (i.e., return to the same position you used to position yourself for the stroke).

Table 3.7 lists some common backhand stroke problems and their results, as well as corrections for the problems.

TABLE 3.7 Common backhand stroke problems.

COMMON PROBLEM	RESULT	CORRECTION
Wrong grip (forehand or thumbs-up grip)	Poor forearm rotation Poor power Poor deception	Use a standard backhand grip. (See Figure 3.4)
Poor forearm rotation	Poor timing Poor power Slicing the shuttle	Rotate your forearm vigorously to ensure flush contact with the shuttle. Loosen your racket grip.
Poking at the shuttle	Poor power and distance	Use a full backswing. Swing hard. Hit through the shuttle. Follow through. Rotate your forearm into the shuttle.
Failure to keep your back toward the net	Poor power Poor deception	Step back with your racket-side leg. Turn your back to the net as you move to the shuttle.
Low point of contact	Poor distance Poor deception	Extend your elbow up and away from your body. Reach for the shuttle.

Drill #12: Stroke Practice for Overhead Backhand Shots

This drill is meant to let you practice each phase of the stroke without actually hitting a shuttle. Instead, the focus should be on producing the appropriate stroke mechanics. For right-handers (reverse for left):

1. Start in the ready position, feet parallel to the net, racket up, and knees slightly bent.
2. Turn your shoulders to the left, step back, make sure your back is facing the net, and bring your racket to the ready position. Hold this position for 2 seconds.
3. Start the backswing, rotate your forearm, and cock your wrist, but do this very slowly (almost in slow motion). Make sure the elbow is up. Pause for 1 or 2 seconds before proceeding.
4. Slowly, again almost in slow motion, start the swing. Bring your elbow up and out. Focus on keeping the elbow up, extending your arm, and reaching as high and out as possible while maintaining a slight elbow bend. Watch your forearm rotate and the wrist become uncocked as you imagine contact with the shuttle. Make sure that your weight is on the right leg, which should be deep in the court facing away from the net.
5. Complete the follow-through with your arm pointed toward the right sideline. Push off with your right leg as you turn to your right and return to the ready position.

CUE: Try to emulate the drawings in Figure 3.25 during each of the different phases of the stroke. It might also help working with a partner who can tell you if you are doing something wrong.

Drill #13: Continued Stroke Practice

As you become more comfortable with the stroke, conduct the same drill but without a pause in the stroke, except between the ready and the preparation phase. Most players will hold the preparation phase for a short time as they wait for the shuttle. As you become better, use a small hop to transfer from the ready phase to the preparation phase. Practice starting your swing early, so contact can be made with the shuttle at the same time your right foot makes contact with the floor. Concentrate on the same points as discussed above, trying to perfect the stroke motion.

Drill #14: Add Movement

Start in the middle of the court, then move backward for two steps before initiating the stroke. Concentrate on completing the stroke in one smooth motion at the completion of your movement. Return to the middle of the court at the completion of your follow-through; then start over.

CUE: As with drill #1, it helps if you try to emulate the positions shown in Figure 3.25. Work with a partner who can give you feedback on what you are doing right or wrong.

Drill #15: Add a Shuttle

Have a partner stand on the opposite side of the net, facing you. Your partner will then hit a shuttle to your backhand side, and you will execute the stroke and hit the shuttle over the net. See Figure 3.12 on the forehand drills for approximate placement of yourself and your partner. At this point, it is most important to think about executing the stroke appropriately; do not worry about where you hit the shuttle.

1. Start with a slow swing, concentrating on executing a full backswing and the correct mechanics of the swing. The shuttle will not be hit very far, but do not worry about that.

2. Have your partner observe your stroke and give you hints, (i.e., Was your backswing complete? Did you turn your shoulders? Did you reach up for the shuttle? Did you transfer your weight to your right leg?).

3. As you become more comfortable, speed up the swing and concentrate on hitting the shuttle harder. Aim to hit it high and deep.

4. After 10 to 15 hits, switch court positions with your partner, and help him/her to hit backhand shots. You can learn a substantial amount from watching and helping each other.

CUE: Do not worry about where you hit the shuttle at this point. You should concentrate on good swing mechanics, getting your timing, and making solid contact with the shuttle.

Overhead Backhand Clear

As with the forehand, there are both defensive and offensive backhand clears. The object of both clears is to hit the shuttle high and make it land near your opponent's back boundary line. However, because most beginners and intermediate players have some trouble achieving a great deal of power on the backhand side, most cannot master both defensive and offensive clears. Instead, the focus is usually on just performing any type of clear that will force your opponent to go back and hit from deep in his/her court. The focus should be on hitting the shuttle hard, with as much force as possible; do not worry about hitting it over the back boundary line. The contact point should be to the side of your body with the arm extended up and outward, as shown in Figure 3.25. Also make sure that you do not let the shuttle get too far behind you (too far toward the back boundary line); if you do, it will be almost impossible to generate a powerful shot.

Drill #16: Overhead Backhand Clears

1. With a partner, start at opposite sides of the net. The setter will be at center court, and the hitter will start at three-quarter court (depth will depend on how strong the hitter is) (see Figure 3.26 for clarification).

2. Practice the clear by using the overhead backhand stroke, concentrating on hitting the shuttle high and deep. Since it takes a great deal of practice before you can hit the shuttle from end line to end line, it helps if your partner stands near midcourt or closer.

3. Your partner will return the shuttle, using a high defensive forehand clear.

4. As you get better and develop more power, gradually have your partner move back so that eventually both of you are hitting the shot close to the opposite back boundary line.

Figure 3.26

Player positions for the overhead backhand clear drills.

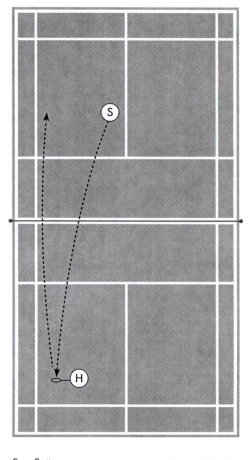

S = Setter
H = Hitter

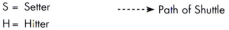

------▸ Path of Shuttle

5. When both of you can comfortably perform the shot, include more movement. Follow your clear to a good receiving position at midcourt. Then move back for the next shot as your partner returns the shuttle.

6. When you have mastered moving to the shuttle and hitting the clear, try to execute 10 to 15 clears in a row without missing or hitting the shuttle out-of-bounds.

7. Switch court positions with your partner so both of you get to practice the backhand clear.

CUES: 1. Power on the backhand clear comes from correct stroke mechanics, timing, and footwork. Thus, focus on positioning your body correctly underneath the shuttle (see Figure 3.25) before initiating the shot; then focus on correct stroke mechanics.

2. Make sure that you extend your elbow and arm up and out (see Figure 3.25) to be able to generate enough power for the clear.

3. Rotate your forearm vigorously.

Table 3.8 lists some common backhand clear problems and their results, as well as corrections for the problems.

TABLE 3.8 Common problems of the backhand clear.

COMMON PROBLEM	RESULT	CORRECTION
Trajectory too high	Poor distance	Adjust the point of contact—you are probably contacting the shuttle too far behind you; the contact point should be at your side.
Trajectory too low	Poor distance (unable to hit shuttle over opponent's racket to make him/her move)	Adjust the point of contact—you are probably contacting the shuttle too far in front or your racket angle is closed. Reach for the shuttle—your point of contact may also be low.
Arm points toward net in follow-through	Poor distance	Be sure your back is toward the net during the swing. Direct your arm toward the right sideline during the swing and follow-through.
Trajectory OK but power poor	Poor distance	Focus on your swing—make sure that your swing mechanics are correct. The most common mistake is using a short backswing and poking at the shuttle. Swing quickly and snap the racket into the shuttle at contact. Focus on your forearm rotation—much of the power of the backhand clear will come from your forearm rotation.

Backhand Smash

The backhand smash is an advanced shot, and few beginners or intermediate players possess the power and timing needed to execute it correctly. Even advanced players cannot hit the backhand smash as hard as the forehand smash. Therefore, when used, it is often hit from half-court or closer to the net after your opponent has made a mistake and hit a poor shot. If used, the mechanics are the same as for the backhand clear except that the shuttle is contacted more in front of the body and the racket head is pointed slightly downward, as in the forehand smash. Thus, the stroke is the same as for the backhand clear, only the smash is hit with a steeper angle. However, it is probably best not to worry about being able to execute the backhand smash until most other shots have been mastered.

Overhead Backhand Drop

As with the forehand, overhead backhand drop shots can be slow or fast. The angle of contact and trajectories are the same as for the forehand (see Figures 3.20 and 3.21). However, because most players cannot generate as much power on the backhand as on the forehand side, it is important to be able to execute good backhand drop shots. Few players hit backhand drop shots with a slice because this makes it more difficult to execute the shot accurately. Instead, focus on contacting the shuttle flush, and use the racket speed and angle of contact to control the drop. For beginners, it is often easier to learn the loop drop shot, then learn the attacking drop.

Backhand Loop Drop

The loop drop is performed by slowing down your swing just before contact, and by executing a very short follow-through. The contact point should be in a position similar to that of the defensive clear. Thus, think about this shot as if you were executing a defensive clear but with a lot less force and power. Power is reduced by reducing forearm rotation (supination). You want to hit this shot so the shuttle drops as close to the net as possible. The straight-ahead drop is the easiest to learn. Try to hit this shot within 12 to 18 inches of the sideline. In a game situation, this will pull your opponent out of position and force him/her to move to the side as well as forward. Cross-court drops are harder to execute. You hit the shuttle cross-court by controlling the contact point of the shuttle. This shot should be contacted in front of the body and the racket head is not fully rotated at the point of contact, thus guiding the shuttle cross-court.

Drill #17: Backhand Drops

1. Work with a partner. Your partner will stand on the opposite court, close to the net, and hit high defensive clears to you. Your starting position should be along the midline of the court, a step or two inside the long doubles service line.
2. Hit a slow drop off each defensive clear (Figure 3.27a). Focus on executing a complete and correct stroke, but slow it down to decrease the shuttle speed.
3. Your partner should let your drops fall to the floor so you can see where they land, which will let you know when your shots are hit in the right spot.
4. After 12 to 15 shots, switch court positions with your partner.
5. As you become comfortable with this shot, hit drops from all positions along the back boundary line. Start with hitting only straight drop shots; then try to

hit some drops cross-court. Your partner should still let the shuttle hit the floor to let you evaluate the success of your shots.

6. After 15 to 20 shots, switch court positions with your partner.

CUES: 1. Reach for the shuttle and make contact at the highest possible point, but remember to reach up and out. Do not drop your elbow and execute the shot with a substantially bent arm.

2. Do not cut back on your backswing. Execute a complete backswing, but reduce power by eliminating your forearm rotation and wrist action. Keep the grip quite firm.

3. Try to hit each drop softly enough so that the shuttle makes as little sound as possible when contacting the racket.

Drill #18: Attacking Drops

The backhand attacking drop is also easier to hit straight ahead, unlike the forehand attacking drop shot. The differences between the attacking and loop backhand drop shots are the speed of the swing, the follow-through, and the point of contact. It is imperative that the attacking drop shot be contacted just in front of the body with the racket angle controlling the downward angle, not the racket speed. Unlike the slow drop, you want the shuttle to snap off the racket to make a similar snapping sound as during the clear.

1. Work with a partner. Your partner will stand close to the net on his/her forehand side and hit high defensive clears to you. Your starting position should be somewhat in the middle of the court but toward the backhand side (Figure 3.27), near the long doubles service line.

2. From your position, hit a fast drop straight ahead (Figure 3.27b). Focus on reaching for the shuttle and popping it as you make contact. Do not worry about hitting it in the court in the beginning. It is more important to get the feel of executing good racket speed and popping the shuttle. As you get more comfortable, increase the racket speed.

3. Your partner should let each shot drop to the floor so you can see where it lands.

4. Complete 12 to 15 shots, and then switch court positions with your partner.

5. When you become better and can hit most of your shots in the court, try to vary the speed of the drop. An attacking drop shot can be hit with different speeds to further confuse your opponent.

6. As you become more comfortable with this shot, try to also hit a cross-court attacking drop (Figure 3.27c). As for the slow drop, make sure that you contact the shuttle high and early, and control the direction by not completely finishing your forearm rotation.

CUES: 1. Reach for the shuttle—do not let it drop.

2. Do not slow down your swing. The more you slow down your racket speed, the more loft you need to give the shuttle, which means your shot will become a slow (loop) drop instead of an attacking drop shot.

3. Snap the racket head into the shuttle (forearm rotation) so the shuttle produces a popping sound at contact.

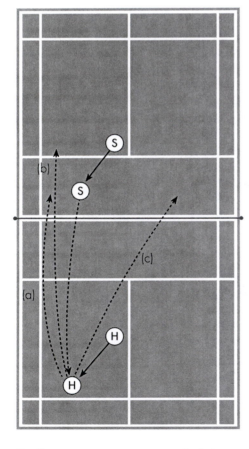

Figure 3.27

Player positions for the overhead backhand drop shot drills: (a) loop drop, (b) attacking drop, and (c) cross-court drop.

S = Setter
H = Hitter
——→ Path of player
------▶ Path of shuttle

The common errors for the backhand drop shots are very similar to those previously listed for the forehand drop shot. See Table 3.5 on forehand drop shot problems for specific problems and corrections.

SKILL 7 | Sidearm Strokes

Forehand Sidearm Stroke

The forehand sidearm stroke can be used to execute drives, drops, and clears, although the most common shots are the drives and drops. Figure 3.28 shows the flight patterns of common sidearm strokes. The contact point is usually between the waist and the shoulders and at the side of the body. Both the drive and the drops are most often used as offensive shots. Sidearm strokes are more common during doubles or mixed doubles play than during singles play. Figure 3.29 depicts the basic mechanics of the forehand sidearm stroke. There are five steps in the execution of the forehand sidearm stroke:

1. Use a standard forehand grip.
2. From the ready position, step to the right with the right leg. At the same time, start the backswing.
3. The backswing should be quick. Extend your elbow out away from your body (about 90°) flexed, with your forearm supinated (the inside of your forearm should point up). Cock your wrist and rotate your right shoulder back.
4. For the swing, start with an upper body rotation, bringing your right shoulder toward the net. Extend your forearm toward the sideline and rotate inward (pronate) and uncock your wrist, allowing flush contact with the shuttle.
5. In the follow-through, continue to rotate your forearm and uncock your wrist. Your arm and the racket will end pointing toward the net.

The type of shot that is hit from the sidearm stroke is controlled by the speed of the swing, the racket angle at contact, and the speed of the follow-through. Drives are hit flat, as close to the net as possible, with a relatively flat swing and follow-through. Drops are hit by slowing down the swing and the follow-

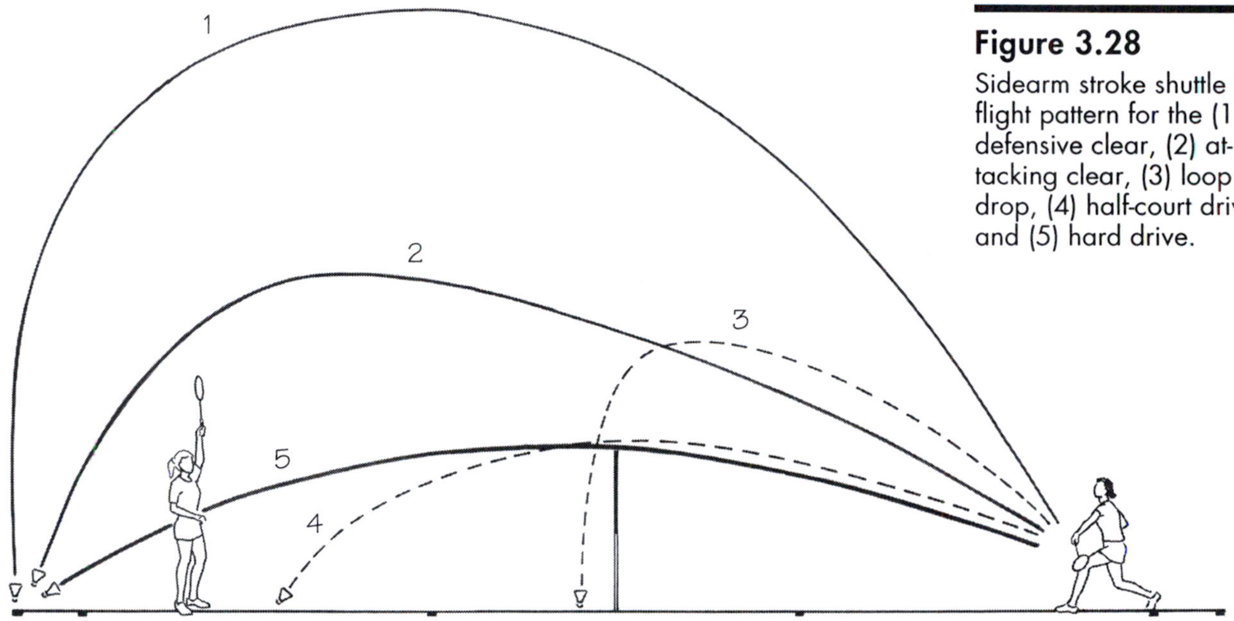

Figure 3.28

Sidearm stroke shuttle flight pattern for the (1) defensive clear, (2) attacking clear, (3) loop drop, (4) half-court drive, and (5) hard drive.

Figure 3.29

Forehand drive movement pattern.

through. Clears are executed by swinging up toward the shuttle and finishing the follow-through in an upward motion. See Figure 3.30 for swing and follow-through trajectories.

CUES: 1. Step toward the shuttle and reach back during the backswing.
2. Make sure that your right shoulder is slightly rotated.
3. Do not let the shuttle drop! Make sure that you contact the shuttle as high as possible.
4. Similar to the overhead forehand stroke, maximum power is produced by quick and powerful forearm rotation and uncocking of the wrist.

Figure 3.30

Drive shot swing and follow-through trajectories for (a) the drive, (b) the drop, and (c) the clear.

(a)   (b)   (c)

TABLE 3.9	Common forehand sidearm swing problems.	
COMMON PROBLEM	**RESULT**	**CORRECTION**
Frying pan grip	Poor forearm rotation Poor power Poor deception	Use a standard forehand grip.
Poor backswing	Poking at the shuttle Poor power Poor deception	Use a full, complete backswing. Swing hard and quick.
Waiting for the shuttle	Shuttle drops too low Drive shots not executed if shuttle too low	Step toward the shuttle and make contact as high as possible.
Poor forearm rotation	Poor power Poor control	Adjust rotation to allow your forearm to rotate 90° prior to contact. Continue rotation another 90° during the follow-through. Shuttle contact should be flush.

Table 3.9 lists common forehand sidearm swing problems, as well as their results and possible corrections.

Drill #19: Stroke Practice

This drill will let you focus on appropriate stroke mechanics without actually hitting a shuttle.

1. Start in the ready position.
2. Step toward the sideline and turn your shoulders slightly.
3. Start the backswing by extending your elbow out, supinate the forearm, and cock the wrist back. Do this slowly and hold for 2 seconds in the cocked position.
4. Slowly start the swing. Start by rotating your shoulders, and then extending your elbow. The elbow should lead, pointing toward the shuttle. Extend your arm, rotate your forearm, and uncock your wrist.
5. Complete the follow-through with your forearm directed toward the net, and push off your right leg to get back into the ready position.
   (*Hint:* Try to emulate the drawing in Figure 3.29 during each of the different phases of the stroke. It might also help to work with a partner who can tell you if you are doing something wrong.)
6. Complete the drill without any pause, and add some movement by starting at midcourt.

Drill #20: Add a Shuttle

1. Stand at midcourt and have your partner stand in the center of the odd court on the other side of the net. Your rackets should be lined up (see Figure 3.31). You can now both execute the forehand sidearm stroke with straight-ahead hits. To

Figure 3.31

Forehand sidearm drill court positions for (a) the drive, and (b) the drop.

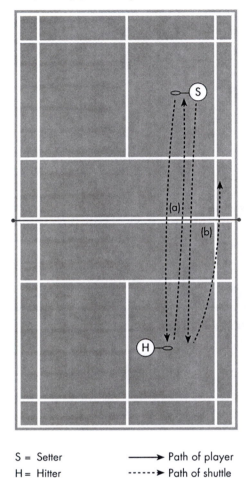

S = Setter → Path of player
H = Hitter ----▶ Path of shuttle

practice the sidearm drive shot, hit the shuttle back and forth with a controlled motion, and try to hit the shuttle flat (i.e., keep it relatively close to the net). As you become more comfortable with the stroke, focus on hitting harder.

2. To practice the drop shot, after 3 to 4 drives, hit a drop (see Figure 3.31b). Your partner should let it drop to the floor so you can get an idea of where it lands and to judge how hard you need to hit. Alternate with your partner as to who will hit the drop shot.

3. To practice the clear, after 3 to 4 drives, hit a clear instead of a drive. Your partner should let the shuttle drop to let you see where the shuttle lands. Alternate with your partner as to who will hit the clear.

Backhand Sidearm Stroke

The backhand sidearm stroke can also be used to execute drives, drops, and clears, although the most common shots are the drives and drops. The flight patterns are the same as for the forehand sidearm strokes (see Figure 3.28). The contact point is also between the waist and the shoulders on the backhand side of the body. Because most players lack power on the backhand side, the most common shots are the half-court drive and the drop shots. However, good players will be able to execute all the same shots from the backhand side as well as the forehand side. The basic mechanics for the backhand sidearm stroke are as follows (Figures 3.32a and 3.32b).

1. Use the thumbs-up backhand grip and stand in the ready position.

2. In preparation, turn your non-racket shoulder back and step with the racket-side leg toward the backhand sideline.

3. For the backswing, lift your elbow and point it toward the oncoming shuttle and rotate your forearm inward (palm down). The racket head should be above the level of the wrist.

Figure 3.32a

High backhand drive movement pattern.

Figure 3.32b
Low backhand drive movement pattern.

4. For the swing, extend your elbow, rotate your forearm outward (supinate), and extend your wrist. The racket head should be flush with the shuttle at contact.

5. In the follow through, the racket head should be up, and the shaft of the racket should be pointed toward the net. Push off your racket-side leg and rotate back into the ready position.

CUES: 1. Step toward the shuttle, and prepare the backswing.

2. Keep your elbow up and pointed toward the shuttle.

3. Rotate your forearm. Most of the power comes from extending the elbow and proper forearm rotation.

4. In the follow through, end up in the ready position.

Table 3.10 lists some common backhand sidearm stroke problems, as well as their results and possible corrections.

Use the same drills as for the forehand sidearm strokes (see Figure 3.31).

TABLE 3.10 Common problems on the backhand sidearm stroke.

COMMON PROBLEM	RESULT	CORRECTION
Using the wrong grip	Poor power Poor control Poor deception	Use the thumbs-up backhand grip.
Using the wrist to execute the shot	Poor power Poor control	Do not use wrist extension to execute the shot—extend your elbow and rotate your forearm vigorously to generate power.
Dropping the elbow	Poor power Poor control Poor deception	Keep your elbow up—it should be in line with and pointed toward the shuttle.

SKILL 8   Underhand Strokes

There are two basic underhand shots: clears and drops. They can be executed both on the forehand and backhand sides. Underhand clears are used when a player has been pushed out of position and the opponent hits a drop shot that can barely be reached. This is usually a defensive shot, hit below the waist with a high upward trajectory. The basic premise is to execute this shot just like any defensive clear: to restart the rally by hitting the shuttle high and deep to the back boundary line and, as a result, get the time to position yourself in the ready position at midcourt. However, sometimes this can also be an offensive shot. If you read your opponent's shot and can get a jump on the shuttle, racket contact can occur above waist level. This will cause your opponent to pause, then as he/she steps toward the net (thinking you will execute a drop shot), quickly flick the shuttle over your opponent's head.

Underhand drop shots (or **push shots**) are executed from a similar position, close to the net after your opponent has hit a drop shot, but without full racket motion. Instead, the shuttle is contacted very lightly to gently drop it back over the net, as close to the **net tape** as possible. This will force your opponent out of position and may often yield a winner. The key to the underhand drop shot is to contact the shuttle as high and as early as possible both to decrease the shuttle travel time and to make it more difficult for your opponent to return the shot.

Smashes are often returned with underhand strokes. From near midcourt, smashes can be returned with underhand clear, drive, or drop shots.

push shot A soft shot hit with little racket motion from the forecourt to the opponent's forecourt or midcourt; often used to hit doubles service returns.

net tape The white strip marking the top of the net.

Forehand Underhand Clear

There are six steps in executing a forehand underhand clear (for right-handers; reverse for left):

1. From the ready position, step forward on your right leg while flexing the knee to about 90°.
2. Point the toe toward the oncoming shuttle.
3. Use a loose grip.
4. Try to keep your right elbow positioned above your right knee (Figure 3.33c–e).
5. Uncock your wrist using a sweeping racket motion, with forearm pronation and elbow flexion (see Figure 3.33d–e).
6. Follow through by extending the racket in the direction of the desired trajectory.

CUES: 1. Step forward on your *right* leg—try to get to the shuttle as early as possible.
2. Racket preparation is a key. Keep the racket in the ready position, with the racket head to the side of your body, as shown in Figure 3.33.
3. Exaggerate the follow-through slightly.
4. Push off your right leg to get back into the ready position.

Drill #21: Stroke Practice

This drill is meant to let you practice each phase of the stroke without actually hitting a shuttle. Instead, focus on producing the appropriate stroke mechanics. If right-handed:

1. Start in the ready position, feet parallel to the net, racket up, and knees slightly bent.
2. Turn slightly to your forehand side, as if the shuttle was just dropped close to the net on your forehand side and you are watching it.

(a) (b) (c)

(d) (e)

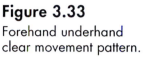

Figure 3.33
Forehand underhand clear movement pattern.

3. Step toward the net with your left leg.
4. Take a lunging step with your right leg, as shown in Figure 3.33.
5. Make sure the racket is parallel to the floor in the ready position, as shown in Figure 3.33. Hold this position for 1 to 2 seconds.
6. Swing through (see Figure 3.33e), and push off your right leg to get back into the ready position.
7. As you become comfortable with the footwork and the stroke, execute the entire sequence without a pause.

Drill #22: Add a Shuttle

Have your partner stand on the other side of the net. See Figure 3.34 for approximate placement. Your partner will toss the shuttle, simulating a drop shot. You will execute the underhand clear.

1. Start from the ready position and concentrate on stepping with the non-racket leg, then lunging with the racket leg.
2. Execute the shot. Concentrate on contacting the shuttle flush and hitting high. Don't worry about where it lands in the beginning.
3. As you become more comfortable, speed up your motion and concentrate on hitting the shuttle high and deep. Try to hit it within 1 foot of the back boundary line.
4. After 8 to 10 shots, switch court positions with your partner, and then continue switching back and forth after every 8 to 10 shots.

CUE: 1. Use your feet! The earlier you can contact the shuttle, the better off you are. Do not wait for the shuttle to come to you, but really try to move to it! This will allow you to produce a flatter trajectory; flick the shuttle over your opponent's head. As you get better at this, try to contact the shuttle as

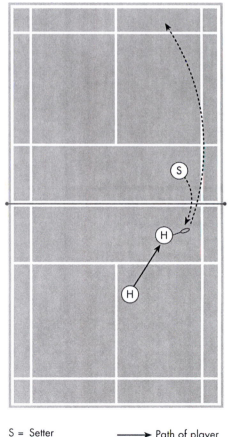

Figure 3.34
Player positions for the forehand underhand drills.

S = Setter
H = Hitter

——▶ Path of player
- - - -▶ Path of shuttle

high as possible, within 1 foot of the top of the net. Then try to quickly flick it into the backcourt.

2. To promote consistency, lunge to the net (shuttle contact point) so your racket elbow is always above your racket knee.

Backhand Underhand Clear

There are eight steps in executing the backhand underhand clear. If right-handed:

1. Step forward on your right leg—bend the knee to about 90°.
2. Point the toe toward the shuttle.
3. Use a loose thumbs-up backhand grip.
4. Lunge to the net with your right elbow at a point over your right knee. The elbow should be flexed 90°, and you should lead with your forearm.
5. Cock your wrist and pronate your forearm.
6. Use a sweeping racket motion, similar to the forehand shot (Figure 3.35). Keep your elbow flexed until just before contact.
7. As you uncock your wrist, rotate your forearm and extend the elbow forcefully into the shuttle at contact.
8. Follow through by extending the racket in the direction of the desired trajectory.

CUES: 1. Step forward on your right leg—both the forehand and backhand underhand clears are hit from the right leg.
2. Prepare the racket early—start racket preparation as you step toward the shuttle.
3. Use your feet—get to the shot as early as possible.
4. The power comes from forearm rotation, elbow extension, and un-cocking the wrist.
5. Follow through in the direction you wish to hit the shuttle.

Drill #23: Stroke Practice

This drill is meant to let you practice each phase of the stroke without actually hitting a shuttle. Instead, focus on producing the appropriate stroke mechanics. If right-handed:

Figure 3.35
Backhand underhand clear movement pattern.

1. Start in the ready position, feet parallel to the net, racket up, and knees slightly flexed.
2. Turn slightly to your backhand side, as if the shuttle was just dropped close to the net on your backhand side and you are watching it.
3. Step toward the net with your left leg.
4. Take a lunging step with your right leg, as shown in Figure 3.35.
5. Make sure the racket is parallel to the floor in the ready position, as shown in Figure 3.35. Hold this position for 1 to 2 seconds.
6. Swing through with a low-to-high racket motion, as explained above, and push off your right leg to get back into the ready position.
7. As you become comfortable with the footwork and the stroke, execute the entire sequence without a pause.

Drill #24: Add a Shuttle

Have your partner stand on the other side of the net (see Figure 3.31b for approximate placement). Your partner will toss the shuttle, simulating a drop shot. You will execute the underhand clear. If right-handed:

1. Start from the ready position, and concentrate on stepping with the left leg, then lunging with the right leg.
2. Execute the shot. Concentrate on contacting the shuttle flush and hitting high. Don't worry about where it lands in the beginning.
3. As you become more comfortable, speed up your motion and concentrate on hitting the shuttle high and deep. Try to hit it within 1 foot of the back boundary line.
4. After 8 to 10 shots, switch court positions with your partner; then continue switching back and forth after every 8 to 10 shots.

Table 3.11 lists some common underhand clear shot problems, as well as their results and possible corrections.

TABLE 3.11 Common underhand clear shot problems.

COMMON PROBLEM	RESULT	CORRECTION
Racket grip too tight	Poor control Poor power	Loosen your grip; relax your hand, without making the grip floppy.
Poor timing	Poor power Poor control Causes you to use an exaggerated arm push Poor deception	Synchronize your wrist action, forearm rotation, and elbow extension.
Hitting off the wrong leg	Poor timing Poor power Poor control Can't reach far enough to hit the shuttle	Always hit underhand clears off your racket-side leg (i.e., your right leg if you are right-handed).

SKILL 9 | Hairpin Drop Shots

The hairpin drop shot travels the trajectory of a hairpin close at net. It is a critical shot for singles so that you can pull the opponent all the way up to the net. It is important in doubles when the player is unable to catch the shuttle soon enough to hit it down.

Forehand Hairpin Drop

There are five steps in executing the forehand hairpin drop:

1. In preparation, hold the racket high (between your waist and chest), extended in front and to the racket side of you, with a slight elbow bend and cocked wrist (Figure 3.36).

2. Lunge to the net, landing on your racket-side leg (same leg and elbow position as for the underhand clear). Point the toe toward the shuttle.

3. For the swing, with your wrist cocked, use a very small, quarter-circle motion to contact the shuttle (see Figure 3.36).

4. Use a small follow-through in the direction of the shot.

5. The face of the racket should be parallel with the floor when hitting the shuttle.

CUES: 1. Use your feet—contact the shuttle as high as possible.

2. Firmly plant your right foot just before contact.

3. Start your racket preparation early!

4. Do not uncock your wrist—follow through by slightly extending your elbow.

5. Try to touch and feel the shuttle over the net.

6. Bring the racket back to a high position immediately after the follow-through (see Figure 3.36).

Figure 3.36
Forehand underhand hairpin drop movement pattern.

Backhand Hairpin Drop

There are four steps in executing the backhand hairpin drop:

1. In preparation, hold the racket high, between your waist and chest. Extend the racket forward and across your body (bring your racket arm across your body), with a slight elbow bend (Figure 3.37).
2. Lunge to the net landing on your racket-side leg, with your racket elbow aligned over your racket-side knee. Point your toe toward the shuttle.
3. With your wrist cocked and your forearm pronated, use elbow extension and a very small, quarter-circle motion to contact the shuttle (see Figure 3.37).
4. Use a small follow-through in the direction of the shot.

CUES:
1. Use your feet—contact the shuttle as high as possible.
2. Firmly plant your racket-side foot just before contact.
3. Start your racket preparation early!
4. Gently guide the shuttle over the net.
5. Use a slight follow-through by extending your arm a little.
6. Bring the racket back to a high position immediately after completing the follow-through.

Use the same drills for the hairpin drop shots as for the underhand clears, substituting the hairpin drop for the clears. The footwork and the lunge will be the same (see Figure 3.34); the only differences are the actual stroke and shuttle placement.

Table 3.12 lists some common hairpin drop problems, as well as their results and possible corrections.

Figure 3.37
Backhand underhand hairpin drop movement pattern.

TABLE 3.12 Common hairpin drop problems.

COMMON PROBLEM	RESULT	CORRECTION
Having your body too close to the net	Swing inhibited Poor control	Establish correct lunge landing point (where the racket can barely touch the net).
Using wrist action to hit the shuttle	Poor control Trajectory too high	Hit the shuttle with racket motion from elbow extension.
Pulling back the racket too soon	Shuttle dying on the racket	Use a small quarter-circle swing. Follow through. Make sure that your body's momentum is forward until the shuttle has been hit.

SKILL 10 | Service Strokes

High Deep Serve (Long Singles Serve)

The high deep serve is used primarily in singles play and is a very important shot. The object is to serve the shuttle as high and deep as possible without hitting it out-of-bounds. Furthermore, ideally you want the shuttle to drop straight down as your opponent executes the return. This prevents your opponent from getting a clean easy hit on the shuttle base and makes the return a little more difficult. If the serve is not deep enough, your opponent can take advantage and either hit return shots for outright winners or hit shots that will put you on the defensive. Since you can score a point only on your own serve, it is important that you serve well. Remember that the serve starts the rally, but it is not often a shot that will be a winner. There are six steps to executing a high deep serve. If right-handed:

1. For the stance, stand 3 to 4 feet in back of the short service line, as close to the center line as you can without touching it (if you step on the line, it is a **foot fault**). Put your left foot forward, and spread your feet comfortably apart (Figure 3.38a).
2. On the right service court, the left foot should nearly be parallel to the center line while the right foot will be at about a 45° angle to the center line. The stance is similar on the left service court except that the left foot turns slightly to point at the opposing left service court. Begin with a wide stance, knees slightly bent, weight on the back foot.
3. Hold the shuttle at the base (not feathers) in between the thumb, index finger, and third finger. Flex your left elbow and toss the shuttle to about shoulder height, about 2 to 3 feet in front of you and about 1 foot to the right side of your body (Figure 3.38b and e). If you extend your racket in front of you (just to the side of your right leg), the shuttle should land on the racket face.
4. For the backswing, start the racket behind your body, pointed up with a bent right elbow and cocked wrist (Figure 3.38c).
5. For the swing, shift your weight forward to your left foot. Sweep the racket head in a low-to-high path. Pronate your forearm, uncock your wrist, and "explode" into the shuttle at contact (Figure 38d–e).

foot fault Illegal placement or movement of a player's foot during the service. See Law 14c.

Figure 3.38
The high deep (or the long singles) serve stroking pattern.

(a)　　　(b)　　　(c)　　　(d)

(e)　　　(f)　　　(g)　　　(h)

6. Follow through with your racket head over your left shoulder (Figure 3.38f and h).

CUES:　1. Point your left shoulder toward the net as you get ready to toss the shuttle.

2. Rotate your upper body by bringing your right shoulder toward the net as you start the swing.

3. Transfer your weight from the right to the left foot as you swing.

4. Contact the shuttle just below waist height with strong wrist action and forearm rotation.

5. Exaggerate the follow-through with the racket head carrying over your left shoulder.

Drill #25: Stroke Practice

Practice the serve without a shuttle.

1. Focus on proper weight change, shoulder turn, and racket motion.

2. Make sure you follow through appropriately (see Figure 3.38 for the proper steps).

3. Have a partner watch you and make suggestions if there are any obvious problems with your stroke.

Drill #26: Practice the Toss

1. Keep tossing the shuttle until you have become comfortable and consistent.
2. Then add the swing, but only to point of contact.
3. Toss the shuttle and swing normally to see if the shuttle contacts the racket head without your having to make any adjustments (having to chase or reach for the shuttle).

Drill #27: Add a Shuttle

1. Try to serve as high and deep as possible. Start by trying to achieve the right length. An ideal serve will land 4 to 5 inches inside the back boundary line. An acceptable serve will land between the long service line for doubles and the back boundary line.
2. After you can consistently achieve the right distance, focus on serving higher, while keeping the same distance. A good serve is high enough to drop straight down. Aim for 10 straight high deep serves that land between the long service line for doubles and the back boundary line.

Table 3.13 lists some common high deep (or long singles) service problems, as well as their results and possible corrections.

Short Serve

T The area of the court near the intersection of the short service line and the center line.

The short serve is primarily used for doubles, but it can also be used at times for singles. The short serve can be executed in either a forehand or backhand fashion. It is unique in that it does not require much wrist action. Stand close to the front "T" to execute this shot. Serves should go diagonally across the net into the opponent's service court.

TABLE 3.13 Common problems in the high deep (long singles) service.		
COMMON PROBLEM	**RESULT**	**CORRECTION**
Inconsistent shuttle toss	Poor swing Inconsistent serve	Practice correct toss placement. Place a target on the floor where the shuttle should land and practice the toss. The toss is a gentle drop, not a throw.
Poor weight transfer	Loss of power and depth	Transfer weight to your left foot just prior to contact.
Poor timing of uncocking the wrist	Loss of power and depth Serve too high and short	Practice timing—use the wrist action and forearm rotation to let the racket explode into the shuttle.
Poor follow-through	Loss of power and accuracy	Make sure follow-through ends over non-racket shoulder.

Forehand Short Serve

There are five steps to executing the forehand short serve:

1. The stance should be the same as for the high deep (long singles) serve, with the exception that you may want to be closer to the "T" when serving in doubles.

2. For the toss, hold the shuttle at the base between the thumb, index finger, and middle finger with the base pointing down. Keep your non-racket elbow flexed but slightly extended across your body, in line with and about 1 to 2 feet in front of your racket-side foot. Drop the shuttle straight down.

3. For the backswing, start with your racket in back or at the side of your body and with the racket head pointed down. Flex your racket elbow, and keep the elbow close to your body. Hyperextend your wrist (cock it) (Figure 3.39b).

4. For the swing, move your entire arm, both through shoulder flexion and elbow extension, to contact the shuttle well in front of your body (Figure 3.39c). Do not uncock the wrist. The shuttle is guided (or pushed) over the net, not forcefully hit.

5. Follow through gently by extending your arm in the direction of the serve. Do not uncock the wrist (Figure 3.39d).

CUES: 1. Do not toss the shuttle. Just let it drop.

2. Watch the shuttle make contact with the racket. Do not look at where you want to hit it.

3. Make racket contact slightly in front of your body, as close to waist height as possible.

Figure 3.39
The short serve stroking pattern (left-handed).

TABLE 3.14   Common problems of the forehand short serve.

COMMON PROBLEM	RESULT	CORRECTION
Poor toss (too close or too far from the body)	Poor control	Adjust the toss to allow correct point of contact. Let the shuttle drop—do not toss it with an upward trajectory.
Floppy wrist syndrome	Poor control	Hold your wrist firm and steady through contact.
Fast or choppy swing	Poor control	Slow the swing and keep the racket speed uniform throughout the entire swing.

4. Use a slow, controlled swing.
5. Do not stop the racket motion at contact—follow through gently and keep your wrist cocked.

Table 3.14 lists some common problems of the forehand short serve, as well as their results and possible corrections.

Backhand Short Serve

Service accuracy will increase if the server can reduce any unnecessary movements and standardize the movements involved in striking the shuttle. The backhand service eliminates the backswing and any arm movement of the hand holding the shuttle. In addition, the backhand serve is hit from in front of the body and is easier to execute than the forehand serve, which is generally hit somewhat from the side of the body. There are seven steps to executing the backhand short serve. If right-handed:

1. For the stance, stand within inches of the intersection of the center and short service lines (at the "T"), with your feet shoulder-width apart; face the center of the receiver's court.
2. Use the thumbs-up backhand grip, the right thumb being placed against the side of the handle, which is parallel to the plane of the racket head.
3. For the toss, hold the shuttle by the tip of one feather between the thumb and index finger of the non-racket hand. This is shown in Figure 3.40. The shuttle is held, not tossed, and you will let go of it at contact.
4. From the above basic service position, you watch the net or your opponent rather than the shuttle during delivery of the service.
5. The shuttle is hit by extending your elbow in a short smooth motion. Do not extend your wrist! The wrist and forearm rotation is used only for drive and flick serves to gain the needed power.
6. Follow through for 4 to 6 inches after contact. This is a short follow-through, but do not eliminate it.

CUES: 1. Use an even, smooth, controlled racket motion.

Figure 3.40
Backhand service motion.

At contact, racket head is obviously completely below the racket hand. Racket contact with shuttle is below the waist.

Both feet in contact with floor during delivery* of serve.

*Delivery of serve starts with first forward movement of racket.

2. Allow the racket motion to start before contact. Do not hold the shuttle too close to the racket head. The racket should swing about 8 to 12 inches before contact.

Table 3.15 lists some common problems of the backhand short serve, as well as their results and possible corrections.

In brief, the low, short service can be hit very accurately and should be the primary service in doubles events. Consistent service can be achieved best by standardizing the backhand service procedures. Drive and flick serves should be used sparingly to provide variety and a change of pace.

DISADVANTAGES OF THE BACKHAND SERVICE

1. It is more difficult to serve in the **alley** without loss of accuracy.
2. It is more difficult to develop enough power to hit flick and drive serves.

alley The 1.5-foot area of the court between the singles and doubles sidelines.

TABLE 3.15	Common problems of the backhand short serve.	
COMMON PROBLEM	**RESULT**	**CORRECTION**
Shuttle contact too low or too high	Poor shuttle trajectory or illegal serve	Adjust the contact point to just below your waist.
Fast or jerky racket motion	Poor control	Use a slow, smooth racket motion.
No follow-through	Poor control Short serves Serves into net	Follow through, for 4 to 6 inches after contact, with the same smooth racket motion as for the swing.

Drills for Short Service

Drill #28: Stroke Practice

1. Practice the stroke without a shuttle.
2. Focus on producing a smooth racket motion, for both the forehand and backhand serve. If you want to learn only one serve, practice the backhand serve.

Drill #29: Add a Shuttle

1. In the beginning, focus on foot placement and striking the shuttle cleanly.
2. Make sure that you strike the shuttle as close to waist height as possible without making it a fault.
3. Practice 10 to 15 serves.

Drill #30: Distance Practice

1. Focus on executing a serve that will land just beyond the short service line. A good serve usually lands within 2 to 3 inches of the line.
2. Serve 10 to 15 times, trying to get a feel for how hard you need to strike the shuttle.

Drill #31: Height

1. A good short serve will travel very close to the net and still land just beyond your opponent's short service line. This time, focus on executing a serve that travels within 3 inches of the net.
2. Keep practicing until you become consistent!

Drill #32: Height and Distance Together

1. Focus on executing the serve well enough that it travels within 3 to 4 inches of the net, but with enough power to land in your opponent's service court.

Flick Serve

The flick serve is a quick, deceptive serve, used to flick the shuttle over your opponent's head when he/she is rushing the net thinking you will hit a short serve. It is used primarily in doubles; however, it should be used sparingly because it is difficult to keep in the court and if your opponent does not rush the net, he/she will have an excellent opportunity to smash the shuttle back at you. You can execute a flick serve from both the forehand and backhand service motions.

The basic technique is the same as for the short serve on both the forehand and backhand side. The only difference is that you will rotate your forearm and uncock your wrist at the very last moment, snapping your wrist into the shuttle to create more power at shuttle contact. It is very important to make this serve look just like a short serve until the very last moment, so that your opponent cannot see it coming.

Drill for Flick Service

Drill #33: Height and Distance Together

Make sure that you are comfortable with the short serve before you start working on the flick serve.

1. To help you get an idea of how high to hit the shuttle, have your partner stand 4 to 6 feet in back of the short service line with his/her racket extended straight up (see Figure 4.4, Shot 3).

2. Produce a service motion that is exactly the same as for the short serve. As you contact the shuttle, snap your wrist and forearm to bring the racket hard into the shuttle.

3. Contact the shuttle at an angle that makes the shuttle go over your opponent's racket.

4. Keep practicing, until you can consistently flick the shuttle over your opponent's racket and keep it from going over the doubles long line.

5. Practice hitting the flick serve into the alley or near the center line until you are within 1 foot of your target.

Drive Serve

The drive serve can also be executed from both the forehand and backhand service motion, but it is usually easier from the forehand side. The objective is to drive the shuttle through a flat quick serve into your opponent's court. This serve can be aimed at the sidelines, but it is often used to cramp your opponent's return by serving the shuttle into his/her body. The drive serve is used primarily in doubles; it is especially effective against opponents who **rush the service.** However, it can also be used in singles as a surprise. The key is to hit it quickly and very flat so as to just clear the net, just like a standard forehand or backhand drive.

The basic technique is the same as for the short serve on both the forehand and backhand side. The only difference is that you will speed up the swing just before contact, rotate your forearm and uncock your wrist at the very last moment, snapping the racket head into the shuttle to create more power. You will also need to adjust the angle of contact to keep the trajectory flat. As with the flick serve, it is very important to make this serve look just like a short serve until the very last moment, so that your opponent cannot read it.

Use the same drills as for the flick serve.

rush the serve A doubles service return tactic to move quickly to attack the opponent's low serve.

SKILL 11 | Blocking Strokes (Smash Defense)

There are two basic defenses in badminton for the beginner to learn. These are the crouch and the standard backhand defenses.

The Crouch Defense

The crouch defense is used by the player who is standing near the short service line at net and who needs to defend a smash (Figure 3.41). This usually happens only in doubles, and it is the normal defense position for women in mixed doubles. Goggles are recommended. There are six steps when using the crouch backhand defense:

1. Employ a wide straddle stance, knees bent, with your weight forward on the toes. Face the shuttle straight on. You should stand on, or near, the short service line.

2. The racket should be up, in front of your body (see Figure 3.41).

3. Hold the racket with the frying pan grip.

4. You need to intensely focus on the shuttle.

Figure 3.41
The crouch defense of the smash shot.

TABLE 3.16	Common crouch defense problems.	
COMMON PROBLEM	**RESULT**	**CORRECTION**
Stance too far back in the court	Angle of smash too steep to return it	Step up and keep your feet around the short service line.
Eyes closed as smash is hit	Cannot see shuttle to return it	Watch the shuttle.
Swinging at the shuttle	Swing missing shuttle	Block the shuttle—do not swing

5. Little swing is required. The momentum of the smash will carry the shuttle back over the net. You can control the direction of your shot by altering the racket angle.

6. Raise the racket immediately after contact in order to be prepared for the return in a game situation.

CUES: 1. Exaggerate the crouch—get as low as possible while still being in a comfortable stance.

2. Be as relaxed as possible.

3. Watch the shuttle!

Table 3.16 lists some common crouch defense problems, as well as their results and possible corrections.

The Standard Defense

The standard defense is used when you are at midcourt and the opponent is about to smash from the back boundary line. There are four steps when using the standard backhand defense:

Figure 3.42

The standard defense of the smash shot.

1. Use a wide straddle stance, with your knees slightly bent, your wrist about chest high, and the racket parallel to the floor (Figure 3.42).

2. Step toward the shuttle, racket foot forward, for both forehand and backhand strokes.

3. Contact the shuttle in front of your body as high as possible, and push or block the shuttle in a flat (or downward if the smash is high) trajectory. This can be either a hard, crisp return or a softer drop shot placement, depending on how much racket motion you use. It is easier to learn a softer block, creating a drop shot off your opponent's smash.

4. Minimal backswing is needed since the momentum of the smash will carry the shuttle back over the net.

CUES: 1. Contact the shuttle in front of your body (see Figure 3.42). This makes it much easier to direct the shuttle where you want it.

2. Use just a slight follow-through. This will make it easier to make sure the shuttle actually goes over the net.

TABLE 3.17 Common standard defense problems.

COMMON PROBLEM	RESULT	CORRECTION
Arm and wrist too tense	Poor returns (too high or into the net)	Relax your arm and wrist—be firm but relaxed.
Waiting for instead of moving toward shuttle	Hitting off wrong leg Low contact point Poor consistency	Move to the shuttle—step with your racket leg for both forehand and backhand shots.

3. Use a thumbs-up backhand grip for all shots hit at your body or on the backhand side.

Table 3.17 lists some common standard defense problems, as well as their results and possible corrections.

Drills for Smash Defense

Drill #34: Stroke Practice

1. Start by having a partner throw a shuttle at you from the opposite front court.
2. As your partner throws the shuttle (from his/her side of the net), direct the shuttle back over the net with a block, as described above.
3. Throw 10 shuttles each to the forehand and backhand sides, as well as right at the body.
4. Change court positions so your partner can hit these returns.

Drill #35: Smash Practice

1. After you have become comfortable with the basic stroke and positions, have your partner hit soft smashes to you. Start by serving to your partner, but only serve to half-court.
2. Your partner can then hit a soft smash to you, and you direct the shuttle back over the net (see Figure 3.42). Again, focus on being relaxed and just block the shuttle back.
3. Try to keep your return close to the net. This will make it more difficult for your opponent to return your shot in a game situation.
4. After 10 to 15 shots, change court positions with your partner.
5. Conduct the same drill as above, but have your partner smash at 80 percent to 90 percent of full speed.

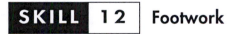 **SKILL 12** Footwork

Efficient footwork is essential for a player to compete at the highest level in badminton. A shuttle is hit every 1 second or less, which means that a player has about 1 second to make a quick start, move to the stroking position, and execute the shot. Similarly, there will be only 1 second to move back into the ready position for the next shot. There are several very specific techniques that are required to move quickly and efficiently about the court.

It is recommended that you focus on stroking first, before working on footwork. After you have become somewhat proficient with stroke production, footwork can be practiced. There are many exercises that can help lead up to efficient footwork. Forward and backward sprints, along with side shuffles, will help build the explosive power in the legs that is required. Jumping rope is one footwork aid that badminton players can do in the gym. Any activity that involves quick, explosive changes of direction can also be helpful. Weight training under professional guidance also is undertaken by serious players.

Advanced footwork is highly intricate and requires more muscle strength and fewer steps. Footwork introduced in this section is designed to show the basic patterns of movement from the base position to the four corners of the court and the return to base position. Do keep in mind that there are other footwork variations. Slight alterations have to be made at times to accommodate the size of the player and the placement of the shuttle. For example, a 6 foot 5 inch player may have to shorten stride at times while a 4 foot 5 inch person may have to add a step here and there. It is important that if alterations are made, you still end up on the proper foot for the final step.

The most important part of any footwork is starting at the correct base position. This is generally near the center line about midcourt. Take a wide, comfortable straddle stance with the knees bent and the toes slightly pointed out (Figure 3.43). The weight should be forward on the toes. Ideally, you should achieve this position every time your opponent is in position to hit an attacking shot. If your opponent is on defense (must hit a clear or drop shot), your base position will be taken with the feet aligned up-and-back as opposed to side-by-side (Figure 3.44b). From this base position, movement to a shuttle should be initiated with a **split-step.** You always complete the split-step by coming out with a small jump to one foot, accompanied by a pivot of the body in the direction to which you want to move. You should jump and land on the ball of the foot farthest from the direction you intend to move. You should now be aligned in the direction of movement, and you can push off hard with the foot farthest from the spot to which you want to move. For instance, if you were moving to the left forecourt, your split-step is a quick short jump from the ready position (Figure 3.43, ready position 2) with the body leaning forward and landing and quickly pushing off on the right leg (Figure 3.45, R1).

When running toward the net, you should always hit all shots off the **racket leg.** Sometimes the distance is such that the final step would be taken with the

split-step *A footwork movement pattern taken just as the opponent is striking the shuttle to provide dynamic stability for quick movement in any direction.*

racket foot (racket leg) *The foot or leg on the side of the body at which the racket is held (e.g., the right foot or leg for a right-handed player).*

Figure 3.43

Base ready position with split-step.

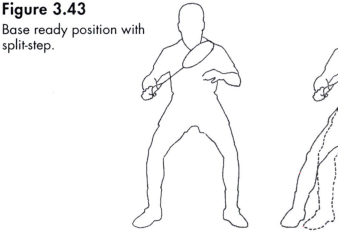

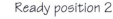

Ready position 1   "Split-step"   Ready position 2

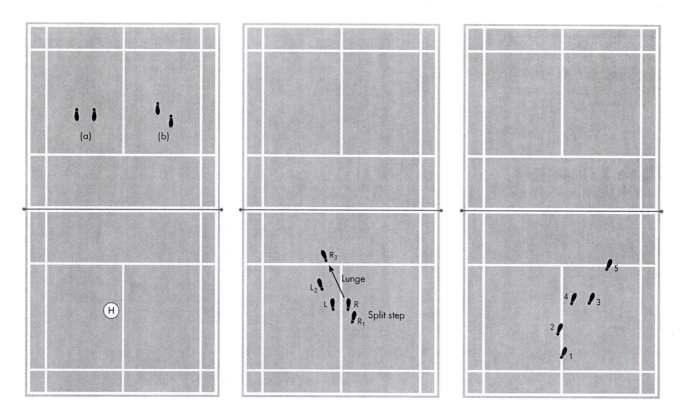

non-racket leg, which would alter the stroke pattern. To prevent this, you should take a *chasse (studder) step* to end up with the racket leg forward. This is shown in Figure 3.46. If step 4 was a full step, you would end up hitting the shuttle off your non-racket side foot. The chasse step, which is a half-step with the non-racket leg followed by the final step with the racket leg (step 5), avoids this. The chasse step can be used when moving either forward or backward. See Tables 3.18 and 3.19 for movement patterns.

Figure 3.44 (on left)
Base position for (a) movement in any direction and (b) up-and-back movement.

Figure 3.45 (center)
Movement to left forecourt from ready position with a split-step.

Figure 3.46 (on right)
The chasse step in moving into the right forecourt.

TABLE 3.18	Footwork to front forehand corner from ready position (Figure 3.47), for right-handers.

STEP	MOVEMENT
1	Split-step, rotate body to forehand corner.
2	Step right.
3	Step left (or chasse).
4	Lunge to net with right leg, execute stroke.

TABLE 3.19	Footwork to front backhand corner (Fig. 3.45), right-handers.

STEP	MOVEMENT
1	Split-step, rotate body to backhand corner.
2	Step left.
3	Lunge to net with right leg, execute stroke.

Figure 3.47 (on left)
Movement to right fore-court from the standard ready position.

Figure 3.48 (on right)
Footwork to return to base position from the right forecourt.

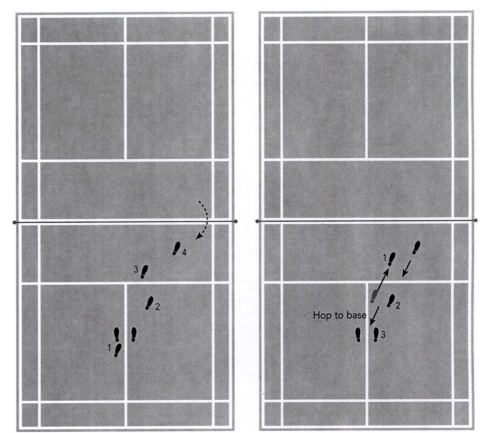

Figure 3.49 (below)
Footwork movement pattern to the forehand backcourt.

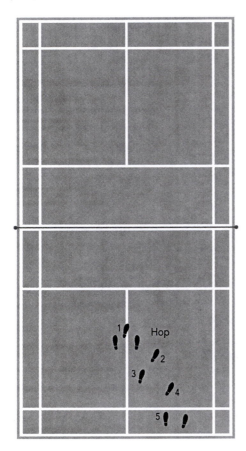

Either of the above movement patterns to the front court could require another two steps, or one step and a chasse if your position is deep in the court.

To return to the base position (Figure 3.48) from the net, you will bring the non-racket leg forward to about 1 foot of the racket foot (1), and then step back with your racket leg (2), followed by a long jump back landing on both feet in a split-step position (3). If you need to move deeper in the court, an additional step or a chasse step can be used between steps 2 and 3. See Tables 3.20, 3.21, and 3.22 for (right-handed) movement patterns.

TABLE 3.20	Footwork to deep forehand corner (Figure 3.49).
STEP	**MOVEMENT**
1	Split-step, turn to forehand side (right turn).
2	Step back (slightly) to right with right leg.
3	Step back with left leg and cross it behind right leg.
4	Step back on right leg and jump to hit shuttle.
5	Land on both feet.
	or
	Rotate left and land on left leg.

TABLE 3.21	Footwork to deep backhand corner (Figure 3.50).
STEP	**MOVEMENT**
1	Split-step, rotate to left (landing on right leg).
2	Step with left foot toward backcourt, with back toward net.
3	Step (lunge) toward backcourt with right leg. Hit shuttle if it can be reached here.
4	Take another left step to move deeper in backhand court.
5	Lunge on right leg, execute shot.

TABLE 3.22	Footwork to around-the-head corner (Figure 3.51).
STEP	**MOVEMENT**
1	Split-step, turn slightly to left (backhand side), but do not turn back to net.
2	Step back on left leg.
3	Step back and jump off right leg. Rotate body to left as you hit shuttle.
4	Land on left leg, push back toward midcourt. (To avoid Achilles tendon injuries, it is recommended that the left foot be directed toward the left sideline to enable shock absorption of the landing.)

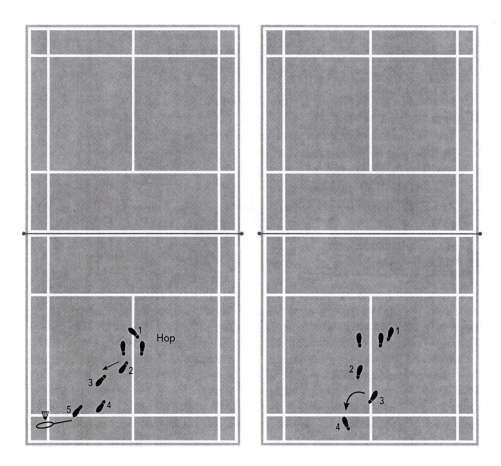

Figure 3.50 (on left) Footwork movement pattern to the backhand backcourt.

Figure 3.51 (on right) Footwork movement pattern to the backhand backcourt to return around-the-head shots.

Footwork Drills

Drill #36: Walk-Through

1. The best way to learn the correct footwork is to start slowly, at a walking pace, without a shuttle being played. Walk through a sequence several times until it becomes easy and natural.
2. Practice each sequence separately.

Drill #37: Half-Pace

1. Speed up each footwork sequence to about half-pace.
2. Don't rush, and go through each sequence separately. Make sure that you follow the proper sequence.

Drill #38: Full Pace

1. Complete each sequence at full pace. This will mean moving as quickly as you can but staying in control.
2. Make sure that you can control your feet and your movement.
3. Complete each sequence separately.

Drill #39: Full-Pace Sequence

1. Start with one sequence, then follow with another one without more than a 1-second break.
2. Complete all sequences before starting over.
3. Do two to three sets of all sequences before you take a break.

Drill #40: Partner-Directed

1. Standing at the net in the center of the court, your partner will indicate which sequence you will perform by pointing to a corner.
2. You will then complete that footwork sequence, and finish at the ready position.
3. As soon as you finish, your partner will point to another corner and you will complete that sequence.
4. Continue until all sequences have been completed.
5. As you get better, try to keep going for 60 to 90 seconds without a break.

Multiple-Shot Drills

Once you have become comfortable with and able to execute the footwork drills discussed above, the only way to become better is to practice. One of the best ways to practice footwork and shots is through organized multiple-shot drills. Through these drills, you will be working not only on shot making but also on footwork and hitting on the move, just like a game situation. Any combination of shots can be used to make up a drill. The following are sequences that are often used. Don't be afraid of constructing your own drills to work on specific aspects of the game. Please remember to warm up well before undertaking any strenuous drill practice. Your warm-up should include both footwork and strokes until you break a sweat.

Drill #41: Clear-Drop Drill

Select which player will drop and which one will clear. Then decide on which side will be the drop side. The player who will drop starts in a ready position at midcourt. The player who will clear starts in a serving position. See Figure 3.52.

1. The shuttle is served high and deep by the player who will clear.
2. Player 2 (the player who will drop) performs an overhead drop shot to the predetermined spot.
3. Player 1 will move to the shuttle and return it with an underhand high clear.
4. Player 2 will again drop to the same spot.
5. Player 1 keeps clearing the shuttle high and deep, and player 2 keeps dropping to the same spot. Player 1 can move the clear around the back boundary line to make player 2 hit the drop from various positions. However, player 2 always drops to the same spot.
6. Switch roles so that both players get a chance to drop and clear. Then switch the drop spot to the opposite side, so that you drop to both the even and odd sides of the court.

Make sure that you execute safe shots, especially in the beginning. You don't want the shots to be so close to the net that they only go over the net every now and then. Execute safe shots with the goal of hitting 25 shots without making an error. The shots will get closer to the net as you become more skilled. This is also good practice for game situations, as most shots should be hit safely in a spot where you are sure that they will land in your opponent's court.

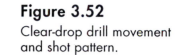

Figure 3.52

Clear-drop drill movement and shot pattern.

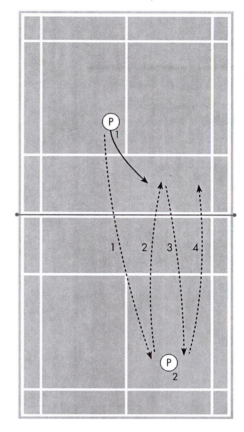

Drill #42: Clear-Drop-Drop-Clear Drill

This is a variation of the clear-drop drill, but it will keep both players moving. This drill is best executed straight ahead and should not involve any cross-court shots. See Figure 3.53.

1. Player 1 starts the drill with a high deep serve.
2. Player 2 hits an overhead straight drop.
3. Player 1 redrops (underhand) straight ahead.
4. Player 2 moves to the net and clears high and deep (straight).
5. Player 1 drops straight ahead, and so on.

This drill will make both players move back for overhead drops, and forward for hairpin drops at the net. It is a great drill for both shots and footwork. Again, make sure that the drop shots (both overhead and underhand) are not too close to the net. You want to become consistent and keep the drill going for about 25 shots.

Drill #43: Clear-Smash-Drop-Clear Drill

This drill is a variation of the clear-drop-drop-clear drill. The only difference is that player 2 will hit a smash instead of an overhead drop shot. The player returning the smash will need to remain in the ready position a little longer and not rush the net too soon. The smash is returned with a block drop shot. See Figure 3.54.

1. Player 1 starts the drill with a high deep serve.
2. Player 2 hits a controlled smash.

Figure 3.53 (on left)
Clear-drop-drop-clear drill movement and shot pattern.

Figure 3.54 (on right)
Clear-smash-drop-clear drill movement and shot pattern.

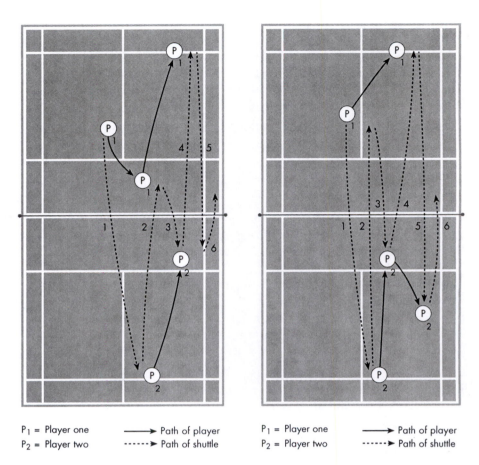

P₁ = Player one   ⟶ Path of player
P₂ = Player two   ·····► Path of shuttle

P₁ = Player one   ⟶ Path of player
P₂ = Player two   ·····► Path of shuttle

3. Player 1 returns the smash with a block drop.
4. Player 2 comes to net and clears (underhand) the shuttle high and deep.
5. Player 1 hits a controlled smash, and so on.

As for the previous drill, make sure that you control your shots so that you can keep the drill going without missing too many shots. Remember that drills are for learning shots, not winning points!

Drill #44: Clear-Clear Drill

This drill will work on your overhead clears. The focus should be on hitting clears that are deep enough to land in the alley between the back boundary line and the doubles service line. Because all shots are overhead clears, this drill can be very tiring. If your clears start to fall short consistently, it is time for a break.

1. Player 1 starts the drill with a high deep serve to the forehand side of player 2.
2. Player 2 hits a straight-ahead clear down the line (Figure 3.55).
3. Player 1 returns with a straight clear.
4. Player 2 hits a cross-court clear.
5. Player 1 hits a straight-ahead clear.
6. Player 2 returns with a straight clear.
7. Player 1 hits a cross-court clear, and so on.

This drill can be somewhat complicated, but remember this sequence: straight–straight–cross-court. The drill is started with a cross-court clear (since the serve goes cross-court). The clears from the backhand side can be executed as either a backhand overhead clear or an around-the-head clear. Don't forget to return to center court after each shot.

Drill #45: Drive Drill

This drill will work on your drives in the same sequence as the overhead clears (see Figure 3.55). The only difference is the starting serve and the players are about 2 steps closer to the net.

1. Player 1 starts the drill with a drive serve to half-court.
2. Player 2 returns the serve with a drive straight ahead.
3. Player 1 hits a drive straight ahead.
4. Player 2 hits a cross-court drive.
5. Player 1 hits a straight drive.
6. Player 2 returns with a straight drive.
7. Player 1 hits a cross-court drive, and so on.

You cannot hit an around-the-head drive, so you must hit both forehand and backhand drives. Start with a controlled, relatively slow drive and gradually increase the speed. This will allow you to gain better control of the drill. As skill increases, players hit all drives from the midcourt position.

Drill #46: Drop Drill

This drill is designed to work on your hairpin drops (Figure 3.56). Only underhand hairpin drop shots are used.

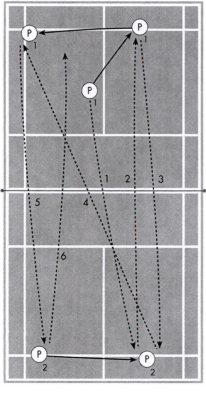

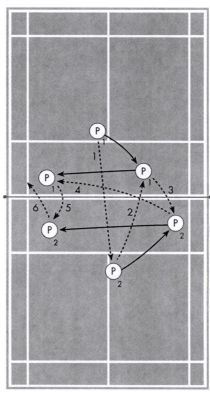

Figure 3.55 (on left) Clear-clear and drive-drive drill movements and shot patterns.

Figure 3.56 (on right) Drop drill movement and shot pattern.

P₁ = Player one   → Path of player
P₂ = Player two   - - -► Path of shuttle

P₁ = Player one   → Path of player
P₂ = Player two   - - -► Path of shuttle

1. Player 1 starts the drill with a short serve.
2. Player 2 returns with a straight drop.
3. Player 1 redrops straight ahead.
4. Player 2 redrops cross-court.
5. Player 1 drops straight.
6. Player 2 redrops straight.
7. Player 1 redrops cross-court, and so on.

The sequence of this drill, starting with the serve, is cross-court–straight–straight–cross-court. Make sure that your drops are not too tight to the net at the start of the drill. The purpose is to get a good feel for the shuttle and the stroke. After several shots, then try to make the drops tighter, but be careful not to miss your shot.

Beginning players may wish to practice Drills 45 and 46 without hitting shot 4 cross-court, but playing onto the rally with straight-ahead clear, drive, or drop shots, respectively. As skill increases the players should add the cross-court sequence.

The above are some of the basic drills that are often used. However, you can design a drill any way you like by stringing a sequence of shots together. It is usually a good idea to work on shot sequences that you have trouble with. Also remember that the drills are excellent formats for conditioning as well as shot practice. If you keep the drill going for ten shots or more, most of the drills will also become conditioning drills. One common conditioning drill is to have one player stand in a predetermined spot on the court (e.g., the deep forehand corner). This player then executes any shot he/she wants. The second player will run down the shuttle and always return it to the forehand corner. This becomes a badminton version of a suicide drill but also focuses on shot making.

Strategies

The biomechanics of badminton stroke production and court movement patterns are pretty well agreed upon by most teachers and coaches. The mental aspects of performance (why was a mistake made) have only been systematically studied during the past few years. Although we can only speculate on psychological aspects of performance, some important considerations for performing at peak levels are discussed below.

PSYCHOLOGICAL STRATEGIES FOR PERFORMANCE ENHANCEMENT

Concentration

Concentration is the ability to selectively direct our attention to sensory perceptions and thought processes. Good concentration allows us to perform as effectively as possible at our given skill level. In badminton, the most important elements of concentration are visual tracking of the shuttle (keeping your eye on the bird), monitoring the auditory cues (hearing sound of shuttle being hit), monitoring proprioceptive perceptions (being aware of your body position and movement), tracking player positions on the court for strategy, and dealing with inner thoughts and feelings (experiencing anger, fear, etc.).

Because badminton involves alternating sequences of play (3–30 seconds) and recovery (about 8 seconds to prepare for the next rally), the player must learn to balance between external and internal concentration processes. During the play periods, attention must be focused on the external cues of watching the shuttle and player positions, to the exclusion of negative internal thoughts and feelings, such as "I must end this rally quickly because I can't win long rallies" or "I am not in shape to play long rallies." During the short time between play periods, positive feelings must be the focus. Rather than negative thoughts about getting tired after a long rally, the player should be thinking, "That rally was really tough; if we play a couple more like that, my opponent will fold."

As stroking skills increase, players learn to hit the shuttle much more quickly and more deceptively. As a result, the opponent must be prepared to move more quickly to retrieve the shuttle. One must also be able both to focus on cues leading to shot direction and speed and to screen out fakes and movements designed to disguise the shot placement. This requires higher-level concentration skills. The player must be mentally prepared to differentiate between relevant cues that determine speed and direction of the shuttle from irrelevant cues that may momentarily delay a quick move or lead to movement in the wrong direction.

Of the external cues, focusing must alternate between gross movement to the shuttle and shot execution. Gross movement involves visual and auditory tracking skills to prepare for quick movement. Shot execution requires quick shot selection and then integration of proprioceptive feedback to keep the body aligned and positioned properly to execute the stroke. Badminton players can play deceptive shots very close to the net or sidelines without making an error as long as they can concentrate and focus on maintaining body mechanics. A great deal of attention must be focused upon selecting shots that are effective strategically and that have a very high percentage of being executed with precision. Many inexperienced players make errors because they change their mind in the middle of a shot and thus are not prepared for effective execution of the shot. These unforced errors play a big part of the game at all levels of play. Some techniques that may help players to concentrate more effectively are outlined below:

- *Warm-up.* Players must be warmed up properly so they feel ready to play. A good physical warm-up brings the player to an appropriate level of arousal and mental functioning.
- *Breathing pattern.* Many players practice deep controlled breathing between rallies. This increases cardiopulmonary circulation and physiological recovery as well as functioning to limit the mind from thinking too many irrelevant thoughts.
- *Relaxed muscles.* Being able to relax the muscles between rallies promotes physiological recovery and reduces overall body tension. This technique is generally coupled with deep breathing (discussed above).
- *Visual concentration.* In an effort to prevent visual distraction from other activities going on throughout the playing facility, many players try to look down and focus on a certain area of the court between rallies. This prevents them from seeing something or somebody and then losing their thought pattern and concentration.
- *Practice concentration.* Practice sessions should include drills of 30 shots without error to develop focused attention during play. Players only become good at maintaining concentration over long periods when they practice these play situations. Tournament players must also be able to maintain focus after they have lost an important rally. Badminton is a fast game, and several points can be given away through a lack of concentration and mental toughness.

Most players try to keep the pace of play fast when they are winning and are focused. When things are not going so well, the player needs to develop some routines (breathing, running in place, mental rhyme) that generally help them to get refocused on the relevant cues of the game and to screen out the irrelevant ones. Players who get angry, worry about losing, or doubt their fitness level often have problems keeping a high level of concentration.

Imagery

Imagery is a psychological strategy designed to improve performance and refocus irrelevant thought processes. This process allows mental images of athletic performance and skills to be repeated, enhanced, and preserved by the brain. Imagery creates and rehearses badminton techniques and strokes in the mind. It involves visualization of play, hearing solid impact of the racket on the shuttle, feeling the soft touch and control of a drop shot, and expressing the emotions of winning or losing a point. Imaging techniques use all of the senses, and repeated rehearsal of these mental processes seems to reinforce neuromuscular function and psychological control of the situation. As a result, imagery is useful in acquisition of basic skills, in refinement and retention of skills, and in development of strategy and confidence for competitive play. Players use imagery techniques when they imitate the strokes of highly skilled players or when they rehearse a strategy to set up a **kill** shot.

kill (put-away, winner) A smash hit to win the rally.

A key factor in the use of mental imagery is that the player must be able to distinguish between a good and a poor performance. It would not make much sense to try to reinforce improper stroking technique if the player did not know the key elements in executing the shot. This could produce play patterns with poor biomechanics that would have to be unlearned before proper techniques could be developed. For example, the rehearsal of hitting the overhead forehand drop shot with the racket elbow low and close to the body would help to establish a movement that would limit accuracy and deception in this shot. Thus, learning would actively be inhibited. Therefore, mental rehearsal should be introduced to beginning players only after they understand and have seen the appropriate badminton skill to be learned.

For intermediate and advanced players who are in the process of refining skills, mental rehearsal should be used in conjunction with physical practice. The technique of emulating the stroking sequences shown in the Skills and Drills section is a form of mental practice designed to increase the learning of badminton strokes and shots. As skills increase, mental practice becomes a more effective technique both for the learning process and for improvement in competitive play.

Mental training can be used as a tool by itself in situations where practice is not possible. If a player is sidelined by an injury, is on vacation, or is unable to maintain a practice schedule, mental imaging of stroking techniques or previous games played will help the player to retain his/her skills and sharpness for competition.

Mental rehearsal is also an excellent technique to prepare for a competitive match. Just prior to an important match, imagery allows the player to rehearse strategies and play patterns to be used. During this process, the player feels the shots, sees the shuttle coming off the opponent's racket, adjusts to a winning tempo of the game, and prepares for the feeling of fatigue that will result from a long and tough match. This pregame process is designed to re-create an atmosphere that existed right before the player's finest badminton match ever.

Mental imaging techniques for badminton can be used to:

- Visualize the basic strokes and cues for efficient performance
- Correct stroking errors
- Replay the strategic play patterns that set up shots to win points
- Rehearse alternative strategies if your initial play patterns are unsuccessful
- Imagine your sensations when your concentration is highly focused
- Re-create how you felt and played in your best match

Although there is no imagery research with badminton players, across other sports imaging appears to be used by the most successful athletes. As players become more proficient, they usually spend more time using imagery techniques.

Stress Management

When players are being evaluated or are exposed to new situations, they often try so hard that they tense up. As a result, their neuromuscular patterns break down and they generally play poorly. They often report that they "didn't know what happened" and really "didn't know why they were losing." These high anxiety and tension levels affected their cognitive function as well as their neuromuscular coordination. Although experienced players are also nervous and tense at the beginning of a tough match, they are able to quickly adjust their arousal level and cognitive function to control the situation and play at their optimal level. In inexperienced players, the anxiety and tension lead to a decrease in performance that creates more anxiety, resulting in a vicious cycle of increasing tension leading to decreased performance. The harder the player tries, the worse it gets. The best way to reverse this process is to utilize relaxation techniques to reduce anxiety and tension.

The most famous and popular relaxation technique is progressive relaxation. It involves lying in a quiet dimly lit room, breathing deeply, and then systematically forcefully contracting and then relaxing each muscle group in the body over about a 20-minute period. This technique served as a model for other tension-reducing techniques such as autogenic training, meditation, and hypnosis. Cassette tapes using variations of relaxation techniques are popular and can be purchased at music stores; they might be helpful for some athletes. One or more of the following six techniques might help the player to reduce anxiety and tension on the court.

1. Make sure the player is sufficiently warmed up. If the player is not physiologically ready to play at a high intensity, a few demanding rallies can lead to breathlessness and uncomfortable feelings, which psychologically increase anxiety and tension. Proper warm-up can often prevent this source of tension.

2. Have the player relax and take slow deep breaths between rallies. Coupled with this, the player should try to relax the muscles. These techniques help to maintain concentration as well as reduce tension.

3. Some players learn to cue on a verbal word (mantra), which helps them to relax. This technique is learned as one becomes experienced with off-the-court relaxation techniques.

4. Maintain a high level of concentration. This keeps the mind focused on relevant performance cues. If players lose focus and begin to doubt their competence or think they might miss a shot or lose the match, anxiety and tension increase and can inhibit optimal performance.

5. Anxiety and tension often occur as a result of pressure to win. This could stem either from pressure by parents, the coach, or teammates or from self-induced pressure. In every match, only one-half of the players can win; in a tournament, only one of many can win. As a result, players should set realistic goals, based on performance, regardless of winning or losing the match. Some goals may be to get every serve in play, make less than three serve return errors in a match, or score X number of points in the game. These realistic goals help the player remain focused and prevent anxiety and tension from becoming overwhelming.

6. Since there is no large prize money in badminton in the United States, most people play badminton because it is fun and they can get a great workout in a short time. If players compete for fun, they should be able to control their stress levels even during competition. If they have fears of playing competitive badminton, they should try to enter competition at levels where their opponents are of similar skill (A, B, C, D, or novice levels).

Goal Setting

Players should set meaningful and achievable goals for the class or competitive season. These goals will provide a high level of motivation, and each success will lead to further motivation to reach the next goal or standard. The following guidelines for goal setting will enhance badminton performance:

- *Goals should be specific and measurable.* The skill evaluations in Section 3 provide specific goals that are measurable for each skill. For example, a goal of serving 5 of 10 shuttles into the target area is a specific, measurable, and achievable goal as opposed to that of serving better, which has no specific measure of success.

■ *Set short-term goals, which can lead to long-term goals.* Setting a goal of hitting 10 consecutive drop shots without error is an intermediate goal to achieving the course goal of passing a test by hitting 30 consecutive drops without error.

■ *Performance goals are more effective than outcome goals.* A player may play his/her best and achieve performance goals even though he/she doesn't win the match against a much better player. Performance goals are centered around skill development and consistency of play. They are most effective in outlining a progression of skill development that is not achieved by a win–lose game mentality.

Self-Talk

Self-talk is a form of thinking or speaking to yourself when you are at practice or in competition. Self-talk can be very effective if it is centered around task-relevant ("Take your time and get your serve nice and deep in the court") and positive mood ("That felt really great") statements.

Self-talk could also work to a player's detriment and cause negative mood states, lack of confidence, and low self-esteem. Such statements as "I don't know what to do," "I just can't hit that shot in," "I never win the long rallies," and "I do not want to play him/her again" are not helpful and inhibit optimal performance. The player must try to substitute such negative thoughts with positive cues such as, "Keep your elbow up in the follow-through," "OK, one point at a time," "I am more fit than he/she is," and "Relax and play high-percentage shots."

Self-talk can be especially important during the following play periods:

■ *To start a match.* Players are often most tense at the beginning of a match. They are keyed up and may not know exactly what to expect. Self-talk cues, such as "Keep relaxed," "Hit simple shots," and "Don't play shots too close to the lines," are effective at this stage of the match.

■ *To stop or prevent a run of points or to keep from blowing a lead.* A characteristic of better players is that they are able to prevent their opponent from scoring a run of three or more points during a service inning. Self-talk cues such as "Make him/her make the mistake," "No more fancy shots," "Hustle to hit a good serve return," "Let's go back to our bread-and-butter shots," and "No unforced errors" are effective in stopping opponent runs.

■ *To close out a game.* Many players have the game in reach but just don't seem to be able to win the close ones. Players often think about winning rather than completing the match. The last shots of a close match are when mental toughness is important. Self-talk during this closeout phase of the game should be directed toward maintaining a focused concentration, playing high-percentage shots, and not trying to be spectacular. Such self-talk as "Concentrate on simple shots," "OK, let him/her error out," "Keep the shuttle in play," and "No fancy shots" is effective in helping to score the final points.

GAME STRATEGY

The basic strategy of badminton is to force your opponent out of position so you can hit a winning shot. The games of singles, doubles, and mixed doubles involve different player court positioning; thus different shot selections and tactics are necessary to achieve the goal of winning. Offense and defense may change back and forth between the players or teams within the same rally. In general, offensive shots are hit downward (smashes, drops, and half-court drives) or quickly past your opponent (attacking clears and hard drives). Defensive shots are hit upward and are primarily clears. Drives are shots that could be offensive if your opponent is out of position. Rallies with many flat smashes and hard drives are called slashing rallies; these shots generally occur before a team establishes the offense or during a transition between offense and defense.

The general tactics a player uses often depends on his/her size, speed, and stroking skills. Three basic styles of players are:

1. *Power.* This player is often physically strong, has very hard and/or steeply angled smashes, and can hit deep clears from most areas of the court.
2. *Counterattack.* This player relies on great fitness, quickness, and agility to retrieve the opponent's shots. The counterattacker may not have great power or finesse but generally wins by forcing the opponent out of position rather than trying to overpower him/her.
3. *Finesse.* This player has excellent racket control and deceptive stroking ability. The finesse player's tactics are to maneuver the opponent out of position with quick, deceptive shots and then hit a winning placement into an undefended area of the court.

Many tournament players have the ability to play all three styles because this gives them more flexibility in counteracting their opponent's style of play and tactics. Regardless of style, players should move to the shuttle as quickly as possible to execute a shot. The ability to hit an attacking shot is dependent upon how high above the floor the shuttle is hit. Players moving and hitting the shot quickly allow less time for their opponents to react to their shot.

In badminton, rallies are difficult to win and easy to lose because of the occurrence of unforced errors. Unforced errors occur when a player hits the shuttle out-of-bounds or in the net when not under pressure. Unforced errors can be reduced by concentrating on the execution of each shot. Players must forget about the last or next rally and focus on the shot at hand. Some players also make unforced errors by trying to hit a spectacular shot or one too close to a boundary line when it is unnecessary.

Playing tactics must also be based upon the fact that points can be scored only by the server (serving team). The server can afford to be aggressive and try some high-risk shots because an error is only the loss of service (**service over**), not a score change. The players receiving service should play high-percentage shots because unforced errors result in the loss of a point.

service over A term meaning the other side gains the service.

Toss for Service

Ideally both sides of the court have equal visibility and no air disturbances to cause shuttle drifts. Often this is not the case, and one side of the court may be much easier to play on than the other. The player or team winning the toss for service has to choose whether the advantage of selecting the side of the court to begin play is greater than that of serving first. Court side is most often chosen in these cases because the best side may be worth several points. The strategy is that if the players are of equal skill, the player on the best side will win. Accordingly, if you choose the worse side to begin the match, you should lose the first game, win the second game on the good side, fall behind in score during the first half of the third game, and end up on the good side for the last half of the game, hopefully overcoming the point differential to win the match. A player with very good deception and questionable fitness may choose the good side first and hope to win easily in the first game. In this strategy, the player hopes to discourage the opponent and maintain his/her momentum and win the match in two games.

Singles is a game that relies on shot consistency, patience, and fitness. The basic strategy of singles is to maneuver your opponent out of the central area (base position) of the court so you have the opportunity to hit a winning shot into the open court. To achieve this, the singles player hits a variety of clear and drop shots into the four corners of the opponent's court. When the opponent is forced out of the base position, the rally can be ended with either a smash or a shot to the farthest corner away from the opponent. The more precise and deceptive your shots are, the less accurate your opponent's returns will be. Once this pattern is established, you need only display patience in choosing the best opportunity to attack and win the rally. Finally, you must have the fitness level required to give you confidence to play the long rallies that are necessary to win in singles. Players who fear getting tired usually take more risks to win a rally and thus make too many errors to win the close matches. Once players become fatigued it is difficult to prevent unforced errors because they must hit the shuttle when they are out of position.

Singles Service Strategy

The serve and serve return are considered the two most important shots of a badminton rally. The basic goal of the server is to place the shuttle in play in such a place as to minimize the serve returner's capability either to hit an outright winner or to control the rally with an effective attacking shot. Consistency and accuracy are the trademarks of an effective service.

Singles Service Position

Most players serve from a position within inches of the center line and about 3 to 6 feet behind the short service line (Figure 4.1). From this position, the server needs to move only a short distance to a base position to anticipate the return of service. It is generally easier to change service position than to change stroking technique to compensate for accuracy of service depth. The server may wish to move forward or backward in the court service area to adjust for serves in which his/her depth is consistently too short or too long, respectively.

The Long Service

The **long serve** is the basic service in singles; the higher and deeper this shot is hit, the more effective the service. This is the most difficult service to return effectively because the shuttle is falling straight down on the back boundary line. For all attacking shots (smashes, attacking clears, and drops), the racket must hit the side of the shuttle (feathers) before the base, thus greatly reducing the speed and accuracy of the return. Therefore, players will generally return this service with a slow (loop) drop or a deep clear. These latter returns give the server much more time to reach the shuttle. To even further enhance the effectiveness of the long serve, it should be directed into the court areas depicted in Figure 4.2 (for right-handed players; reverse for left-handed players). In the even court (area a in Figure 4.2), serves directed to the center of the court minimize attacking returns to the server's backhand and hard smashes down the sidelines. In the odd court (area b in Figure 4.2), any deep service can be effective because the quick attacking clear

SINGLES STRATEGY

Figure 4.1

Singles service and service return positions for (a) the server and (b) the serve returner.

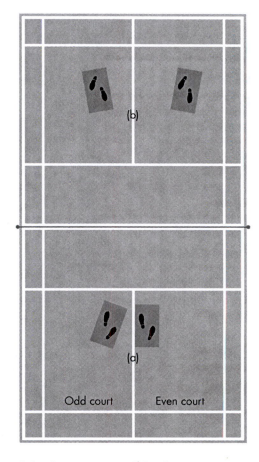

Odd court   Even court

(a) = Server   (b) = Serve returner

long serve A high deep serve directed to land near the long service line for singles.

service returns are directed at the server's forehand. An effective service can be hit against many players by placing the shuttle to the deep sideline of the odd court (area c in Figure 4.2) because it moves the service returner as far as possible from the central base position. This is especially effective against players who lack deceptive cross-court smashes and straight-ahead attacking clears.

Short Service

The short service is generally the first alternative to the long service. This is used for a change of pace or when the opponent has effective smash capabilities from deep in the court. This service might also be introduced if (1) your opponent hits deceptive drops and attacking clears off your long service that you are unable to return, (2) you are serving out of court or have poor depth on your long service, or (3) you want to test your opponent's skill in returning this service.

The short service should be hit with a trajectory to just clear the net and to land just past the short service line (Figure 4.3). Many players do not hit this service with good accuracy and lose control of the rally. When serving to the even court, the prime target area is the center half of the court (area a of Figure 4.3). When serving to the odd court, the entire front of the court can be used with about equal success (area b of Figure 4.3). (Reverse these areas for left-handed players.) The purpose of the wide short service is to anticipate and cut off a low drive to the forehand and hit a cross-court smash return. Because some service receivers do not charge the net to hit a quick or deceptive return, they must return the short service with high deep clears or well-placed drop shots. In this case, the server should be at an advantage. For the slow-charging service returner, the short service should be used but hit much deeper into the court and directed toward the returner's right hip (area c of Figure 4.3). This strategy generally prevents accurate drop shots because

Figure 4.2 (on left)

Long service placements in singles for (a) the even court and (b) the odd court.

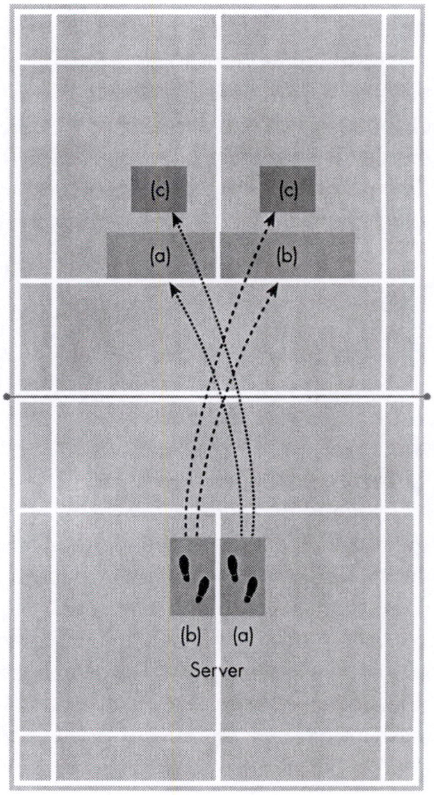

Figure 4.3 (on right)

Short service placements in singles for (a) the even court, (b) the odd court, and (c) the slow-charging receiver.

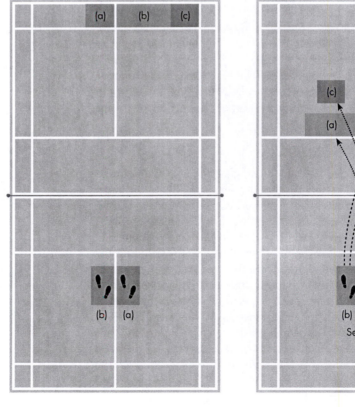

(a) = Even court   (b) = Odd court   (a) = Even court   (b) = Odd court

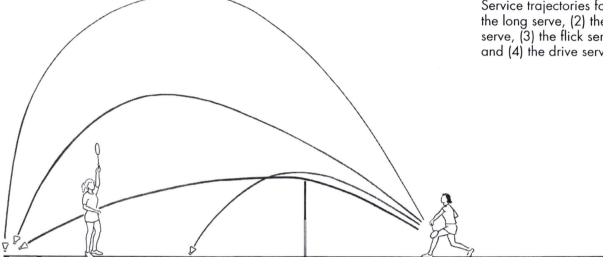

Figure 4.4
Service trajectories for (1) the long serve, (2) the low serve, (3) the flick serve, and (4) the drive serve.

the shuttle must be hit much farther. In addition, drive and clear return shots are generally hit with poor accuracy from this position, which allows the server to immediately gain control of the rally with a smash or attacking clear. A good strategy for the server is to hit the next shot into the service returner's deep corners with as low and flat a trajectory as possible. This should give the server control of the rally.

The Drive or Flick Service

A second but more risky alternative to the long service is the drive or flick service. The drive service is generally directed low and flat, with high velocity, right at the body of the service returner (Figure 4.4). This service often results in service return errors, especially if the returner is caught off-guard or is not concentrating well. However, if the service returner is ready for this return, he/she will generally be able to hit the shuttle away from the server to control the rally. The flick service is designed to carry back to the back boundary line, but with a lower trajectory than the long service (see Figure 4.4). The purpose of hitting this service is to force the returner to move quickly and maybe force him/her off-balance in returning the shuttle, thus reducing the accuracy of the return. The server should be wary of hitting the drive and flick serves in singles to tall players, who generally have effective steeply angled smashes and lots of reach to block shots into the corners of the court.

An accurately placed serve greatly increases your chance to score a point and thus should be practiced regularly.

Singles Service Returns

For the most efficient movement to return the singles serve, the returner should stand with the right foot forward (left foot back) at midcourt about 1 to 2 feet from the center line when in the even court, and about 4 feet from the center line when receiving in the odd court (see Figure 4.1). This position is important because the quickest movement required will be either forward to return a short serve or backward to return a long serve. Correct positioning on the court relative to the sideline discourages servers from trying to drive the shuttle into the receiver's backhand.

The basic serve return strategy should be to gain and maintain control of the rally by putting pressure on the server with a variety of deceptive serve return placements. The objective is to make the server run as far as possible in the least amount of time to retrieve the shot. There are several basic shot selections for the serve return, based on the type of serve.

Return of the Long Service

Long serves that do not have good depth (returned before reaching the doubles long service line) should be smashed down one of the sidelines or right at the racket side of the server's body (Figure 4.5). Since the receiver is hitting a shot with poor depth, there is a tendency to overhit the shuttle and return clears out-of-bounds and drops so deep in the court that they can be returned safely.

Long serves hit toward the sideline should be returned with one of the following three placement options (Figure 4.6): attacking clear straight down the sideline (a in Figure 4.6), straight-ahead drop (b in Figure 4.6), and cross-court half-court smash (c in Figure 4.6). Variability of these returns keeps the server in a base position and prevents him/her from overanticipating shots to one side, the forecourt, or the backcourt. Cross-court clear returns of the long serve (d in Figure 4.6) are risky for inexperienced players because they don't have power to hit it deep and the server's easiest second shot is a drop into the open court straight ahead.

Long serves with good depth directed toward the center line of the court (Figure 4.7) are generally best returned with drop shots to either forecourt corner (a in Figure 4.7), off-speed smashes down either sideline (b in Figure 4.7), and high deep clears (c in Figure 4.7). The angles for hitting attacking clears and hard smashes to pass the server are quite narrow and thus more risky from the center line than the sideline return position, especially if the server is tall.

Figure 4.5 (on left)

Smash returns of the long singles service received in front of the long service line for doubles: (a) straight ahead, (b) cross-court, and (c) right side of the server's body.

Figure 4.6 (on right)

Service return options for the long singles serve: (a) attacking clear straight ahead, (b) drop straight ahead, (c) cross-court half-court smash, and (d) cross-court clear.

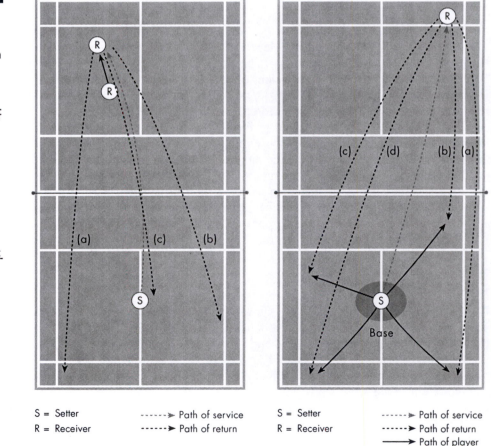

| S = Setter | - - - -▶ Path of service |
| R = Receiver | - - - -▶ Path of return |

S = Setter	- - - -▶ Path of service
R = Receiver	- - - -▶ Path of return
	——▶ Path of player

Return of the Short Service

Short serves can best be returned with drop shots (a in Figure 4.8), drives (b in Figure 4.8), or attacking clear shots (c in Figure 4.8) directed straight ahead or attacking clear shots to the server's backhand (d in Figure 4.8). The most important factors in these returns are hustle and a quick, long reach to hit the shuttle. Don't let the shuttle drop much below net-tape height. These returns should provide the receiver with the attack. The failure of the returner to move quickly to attack the shuttle could result in the quick loss of a point. If the returner is not attacking the short serve well, the best return is a clear, which forces the server back to the back boundary line.

Return of the Drive or Flick Service

Drive or flick serves are very tempting to return with a smash shot (a in Figure 4.9). The smash return creates a quick, slashing-type rally; therefore, the returner must move quickly to attack the serve and then, quickly again, to attack the next shot. Most players who hit this type of serve are skilled at returning smashes and are often tall and hit steeply angled shots to the floor. Another good return of the drive or flick serve is an attacking clear to either deep corner of the server's court (b in Figure 4.9). The server is generally preparing for a smash, and the shuttle usually gets past the server who often hits a weak return, which can be smashed to end the rally. Drop shots and high deep clears are other alternative returns.

An effective serve return requires quick footwork, concentration, and good shot selection. Good returns of service can keep your opponent from scoring many points, whereas poor returns will give the game away.

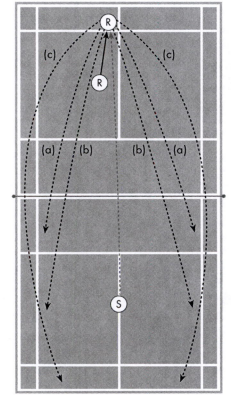
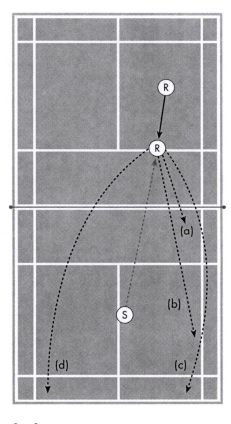

Figure 4.7 (on left)
Return of the long singles serve near the center line with (a) drop shots to the corners, (b) half-court smashes down either side, and (c) high clears.

Figure 4.8 (on right)
Return of the singles serve with straight-ahead (a) drops, (b) drives, or (c) attacking clears or (d) cross-court attacking clears.

S = Setter
R = Receiver

-----▶ Path of service
-----▶ Path of return
——▶ Path of player

S = Setter
R = Receiver

-----▶ Path of service
-----▶ Path of return
——▶ Path of player

Singles Base Position

After the serve and serve return have been executed, the basic strategy is to try to maneuver your opponent out of position so a winning shot can be hit. Success in doing this requires the maintenance of a base position, which sets up quick movement to your opponent's shots and the use of play patterns that force your opponent out of position and to hit a weak return.

After executing the service, the server should take a court position equidistant from the opponent's **power shot** returns (smashes or attacking clears) (see Figure 4.6). The server must also play as deep (far back) in the court as necessary to return the attacking clear and still have time to reach a drop shot or cross-court smash (see arrows for server movement in Figure 4.6). Although this position is deep in the court, it is easier to move forward than backward, and there is more time to return the drop shot than the power shot.

In singles, the entire court can be defended and offenses launched from the base position. The player should return toward his/her center court base quickly and take a wide ready stance or split-step (see Figure 3.43). If there is not enough time to get back to center court, the player should stop wherever he/she is the moment the opponent contacts the shuttle and take a ready position. (See Footwork section.) The only time a player does not try to go back to central base position is after the redrop of a drop shot, at which time the base position moves to the forecourt near the short service line on the same side as the shuttle (Figure 4.10). This prevents redrops at the net, which would reverse the attack, but still allows time to move to the backcourt to return high clears.

power shots *Shots that are hit very hard (e.g., clears, drives, and smashes).*

Figure 4.9 (on left)
Return of drive and flick serves with (a) straight-ahead smashes and (b) attacking clears into either backcourt corner.

Figure 4.10 (on right)
Movement of singles base position to forecourt after hitting a hairpin drop shot.

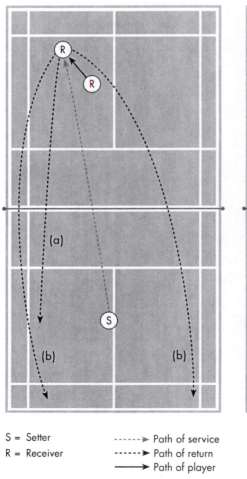

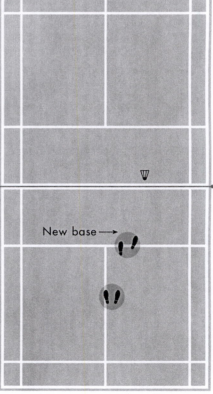

S = Setter	----→ Path of service
R = Receiver	----→ Path of return
	——→ Path of player

Singles Movement Patterns

Singles strategy utilizes a pattern of shots designed to make your opponent run as far as possible to retrieve the next shot. Not only does this tire your opponent, but it also requires the person to hit the shuttle on the run, which allows less time to execute a good shot. Because the court is almost 27 feet long on the diagonal and only 20 feet straight ahead from the back boundary line to the net, it is good strategy to force your opponent to run back and forth from the back boundary line cross-court to the net. The basic movement patterns described below are essential to good singles play.

Tactics to Move Your Opponent to the Corners

There are three tactics to cause your opponent to move.

1. *Run your opponent on the diagonal* (Figure 4.11). A drop to your opponent's forehand (shot 1 in Figure 4.11) followed by a clear to the backhand (shot 2 in Figure 4.11) often forces weak returns (line a in Figure 4.11). This movement pattern increases the likelihood that your opponent will have to play a backhand shot rather than the more powerful around-the-head shot because of the great court distance that must be covered from the forehand net position.

2. *Run your opponent on a broken line* (a in Figure 4.12). The movement distance is about the same as to run on the diagonal, but the direction change requires your opponent to take more time and expend more energy than a straight run on the diagonal. It is also useful against tall players who may intercept the cross-court clear used on the diagonal run pattern. The broken-line pattern can also be forced

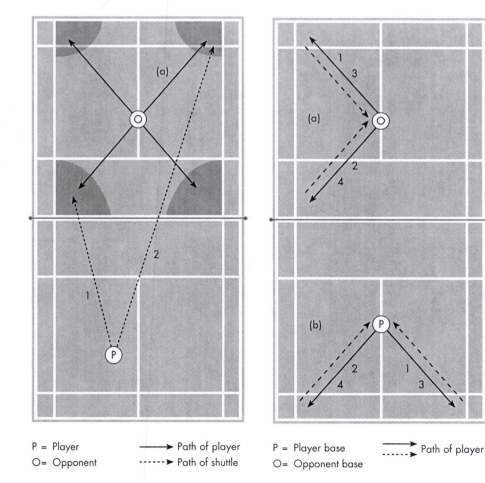

Figure 4.11 (on left)
Shot placement to run your opponent on the diagonal.

Figure 4.12 (on right)
Broken-line corner movement patterns for (a) alternating clear and drop shots straight ahead and (b) alternating clears to the opponent's opposite backcourt corners.

P = Player   ⟶ Path of player
O = Opponent   ┄┄► Path of shuttle

P = Player base   ┄┄► Path of player
O = Opponent base

by alternating clear shots to the opponent's forehand and backhand backcourt corners (b in Figure 4.12). Alternating drop shots to the forehand and backhand forecourt can be useful as a change in pattern but does not require nearly the physical demands of the backcourt patterns.

3. *Use the repeated deep corner pattern.* Hit two or three successive clear shots followed by a net shot. This pattern requires the same distance of the court to be covered but also requires the opponent to reverse direction and go backward again (Figure 4.13). This pattern is physically very demanding. Players should use a combination of these patterns during the rally to make sure the opponent returns all the way to a central base position. Forcing the opponent to run from side to side is not as effective as running on the diagonal because of the narrow width (17 feet) of the singles court.

Tactics to Force Your Opponent to Run Cross-Court

Reversing the direction of play will force your opponent to run cross-court. This is best achieved when your opponent hits a cross-court shot and you return the shuttle straight ahead (a in Figure 4.14). This strategy is very effective because not only does it make your opponent run a maximum distance, but it also gives you lots of shot variety because you are hitting into the vacant side of the court (shaded area of Figure 4.14). In singles, most cross-court shots should be countered with a straight-ahead return.

A second technique to force your opponent to run cross-court occurs when your opponent hits straight ahead and you respond with a cross-court shot (b in Figure 4.12). This pattern requires more precise shot execution and should be used only about 25 percent of the time.

Figure 4.13 (on left)
Repeated deep corner clears combined with broken-line, drop shot movement pattern.

Figure 4.14 (on right)
Run your opponent (O) cross-court by (a) returning cross-court shots straight ahead or (b) returning straight-ahead shots cross-court into the shaded area of the court.

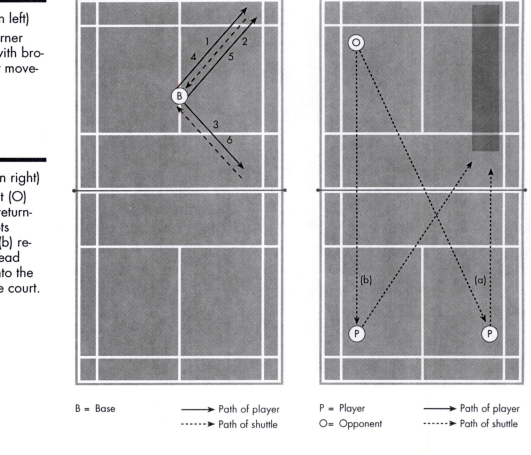

B = Base   ⟶ Path of player
              ------▶ Path of shuttle

P = Player   ⟶ Path of player
O= Opponent ------▶ Path of shuttle

Once the basic shots are mastered and movement patterns are learned, players need to learn to think on the court. With experience, they will discover which shots and movement patterns are successful and which are not. A shot or pattern that wins against one player may not work so well against another. When playing a player for the first time, it is good strategy to hit a variety of shots during the first few rallies of the game so that you get a feel for your opponent's strengths and weaknesses; then develop a game plan for the rest of the match. Scouting opponents by watching them play other matches can reveal shots and play patterns to look out for when playing them.

combination doubles formation *Partners play side-by-side on defense and up-and-back on offense.*
doubles service court *The area to which a serve must be delivered in doubles events.*

DOUBLES STRATEGY

Doubles rallies generally begin with the short service and are followed by a series of low drives and half-court shots until one team is forced to hit a clear shot. When this occurs, the team receiving the clear shot gains the attack and has the opportunity to hit a smash. Once on the attack, they should continue hitting smashes and drop shots until they win the rally.

When a team is on the offense, the players should be aligned in an up-and-back court position (Figure 4.15) and hit smashes until the rally is won. When a team is forced to play defense (hit a shuttle the opponents can smash), the players should defend their court in a side-by-side position (see Figure 4.15). On defense, they should hit drives and drop shots away from their opponents in order to reverse the attack. A **combination doubles formation** is used when partners play up-and-back offense and side-by-side defense.

The Doubles Serve

Men's and women's doubles begin play with both the server and receiver in the forecourt and their partners in the center backcourt (Figure 4.16). Effective serves to the **double service court** enable the serving team to take control of the doubles game (Figure 4.17). The most effective service is the low serve hit 1 to 3 inches above the net. It should be directed toward the "T" (a in Figure 4.17), or toward the service returner's racket shoulder (b in Figure 4.17) in order to create indecision as to whether the service return should be hit with a forehand or backhand stroke. For variety, the short serve can be directed toward the sideline (c in Figure 4.17). Drive serves directed at the returner's racket shoulder (d in Figure 4.17), or flick serves directed toward the sideline or center line (e in Figure 4.17) are often used against opponents who rush the serve effectively.

Doubles Service Strategy

The role of the server in men's and women's doubles is to do the following four things.

1. *Control the rally by getting the shuttle into play* (thus preventing the receiving team from gaining the attack). This is best accomplished by hitting short serves. Drive and flick serves almost always result in the receiving team maintaining the attack.

2. *Control the forecourt by preventing drop shot returns of the service.* This is accomplished by moving to a position in front of

Figure 4.15
Doubles attacking and defensive court positions.

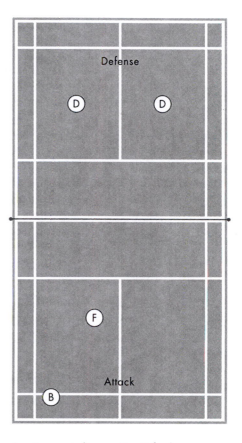

F = Forecourt player   D = Defender
B = Backcourt player

Figure 4.16 (on left)
Basic doubles service and service return positions.

Figure 4.17 (on right)
Doubles service placement (a) to the "T," (b) toward the receiver's racket shoulder, (c) to the short sideline, (d) drives to the returner's racket shoulder, and (e) flick serves toward the sideline or center line.

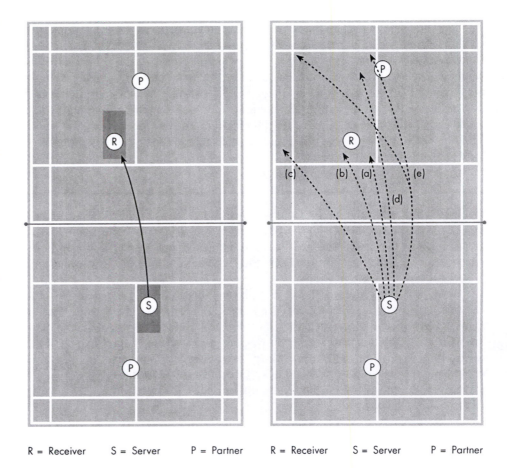

R = Receiver   S = Server   P = Partner   R = Receiver   S = Server   P = Partner

down-the-line shot A *drive shot directed straight ahead down the sideline.*

the receiver and by hitting all drop shot returns above net level with a block shot or a smash. Drop shot service returns should not be returned with another drop because the server will generally lose the attack.

3. *Vary the short serve placement* (depending upon the pattern of returns hit by the receiver). Certain returns are not hit accurately from all court areas. For example, to counter half-court **down-the-lines shots,** direct the serves toward the receiver's racquet shoulder; to counter deep drive returns at or past the server's partner, direct the serves toward the "T." Another good time to try different service placements occurs if your partner is making unforced errors. This change will generally force your opponent to hit a different serve return and maybe result in a more successful return by your partner.

4. *Watch for service return patterns* (once control of the forecourt is established). You might be able to anticipate and intercept a shot for an important point later in the match.

If the above four factors are accomplished, most service returns will be directed toward the server's partner, who should be able to gain the attack with a drop shot, half-court, or smash return.

Choice Between Forehand and Backhand Service Technique

Biomechanically, the backhand service motion is advantageous because it requires fewer joint movements and synchronization. It can also be hit out of a white background (the server's white shorts), thus making the shuttle more difficult to see by the receiver. Most players prefer the backhand serve when playing under pressure and in tournaments. However, it may take time for the beginning backhand servers to develop the necessary power for hitting flick and drive serves. (In mixed doubles, the backhand service for the male is especially difficult because of the deeper serving position.)

The best service, whether forehand or backhand, is one that is hit accurately with a quick, smooth motion. This prevents the service returner from anticipating where the serve is directed until the server's racquet makes contact with the shuttle. Both the forehand and backhand service motions require a great deal of skill and practice.

Additional Service Strategies

There are five additional service strategies.

1. *Standardize your service motion.* Make your service movement pattern similar for the short, flick, and drive serves. Many servers hit the short service while maintaining a cocked wrist and hit the flick and drive service by uncocking the wrist at racket–shuttle contact, thereby creating the additional power to execute these serves.

2. *Challenge the hard service rushers.* Concentrate on executing a couple of good short serves hit at net-tape level. Some players purposely serve the shuttle to land in front of the short service line because the charging receiver will return it anyway and, in this case, from a lower and more difficult return position. If you succeed, your opponent will generally rush less aggressively, which gives you the opportunity to raise your serve 1 or 2 inches to cut your serving errors.

3. *Challenge the serve returners who don't move forward quickly.* Hit low serves at a trajectory to land 2 to 4 feet beyond the short service line. This service will cramp the returner's stroke and force poor service returns.

4. *Don't try to hit service aces.* The accuracy required to hit an ace doesn't leave much margin for error and generally leads to more service errors. Never stop a run of scoring points by serving the shuttle out-of-bounds.

5. *Adhere to all service rules.* See Law 19 of the Rules of Badminton. Make sure you have a legal service motion so you will not be faulted during competition.

Doubles Service Returns

The primary goal of the service return in men's and women's doubles is to hit an aggressive shot so the receiving team can take the offensive and hopefully win the rally quickly. Effective service return technique requires correct court positioning, the lunge, and good service return placement.

Correct Court Positioning

The service receiver should take a position within 3 feet of the short service line. In the even court (Figure 4.18), the receiver should stand about 1 to 1 1/2 feet from the center line to prevent a drive serve to the backhand. When receiving in the odd court (Figure 4.19), the receiver should stand 3 to 4 feet to the left of the center line. The receiver's feet should be about 3 feet apart, with both legs flexed, so the body is in a slightly crouched position ready to either lunge forward to return the short serve or jump backward to receive a flick serve. The objective is to stand as close as possible to the short service line to put pressure on the server while still

Figure 4.18 (on left)
Doubles service return position and left leg lunge in the even court.

Figure 4.19 (on right)
Doubles service return position and cross-over lunge with the racket leg in the odd court.

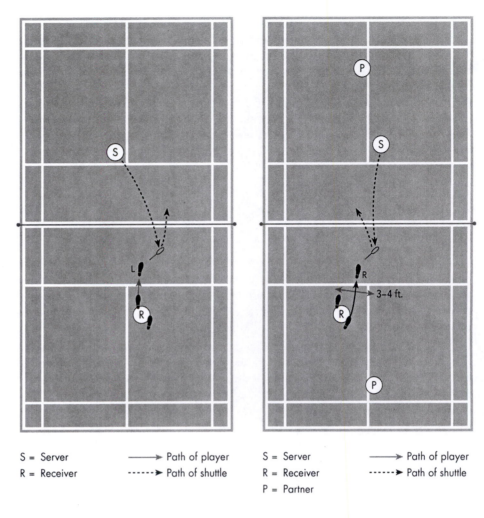

S = Server	——➤ Path of player
R = Receiver	----➤ Path of shuttle

S = Server	——➤ Path of player
R = Receiver	----➤ Path of shuttle
P = Partner	

being able to move backward quickly enough to smash all flick and drive serves. As skill develops, most men and women can successfully return service from about 1 1/2 feet behind the short service line.

The Lunge

The lunge consists of a quick cross-over step from the initial receiving position (see Figure 4.19) with a powerful move toward the net with the right leg. During the lunge, the receiver's shoulders will rotate 180° and the right arm should be extended toward the oncoming shuttle, with the elbow flexed and the racket in a cocked position. This movement places the receiver in the most advantageous position to execute a variety of service return placements to pressure the opponents. As service return skills increase, the returner will:

1. Keep the racket head above the hand in the execution of the return.
2. Keep the racket and arm from dropping below shoulder level during the return and follow-through.
3. Execute the shot at the end of the lunge, just before the right foot lands on the floor.
4. Learn that a hard lunge does not necessarily mean a powerful shot. The lunge and the stroke are separate movement patterns with the stroke occurring at the end of the lunge.

Highly skilled and tall players (over 6 feet 2 inches) often have a service stance with their left foot within inches of the short service line and may lunge with their left leg and exert great pressure due to their size and long reach (see Figure 4.18).

Good Service Return Placement

To return the short serve, a variety of service return placements are used to attack a shuttle directed (1) to the "T," (2) at the racket shoulder of the returner, or (3) wide toward the sideline.

1. The most effective service returns from short serves hit to the "T" area are depicted in Figure 4.20 (shots 1–6). Three of these shots are hit to the straight-ahead sideline: drop (shot 1), half-court (shot 2), and hard drive (shot 3). Two shots are directed toward the center line: drop (shot 4) and drive to deep center (shot 5). Another effective shot is a cross-court drive (shot 6) deep into the opponent's back-hand corner. This return is most effective in women's doubles. Similar shots are hit from the even court; however, the deep cross-court drive is risky because it is hit to the opponent's forehand side where a power shot or straight-ahead drop gives the servers the attack.

2. Serves directed toward the body of the receiver should be returned as depicted in Figure 4.21 (shots 1–3). Use straight-ahead drops (shot 1), and drives into the body of the server's partner (shot 2), or drives into either deep backcourt corner

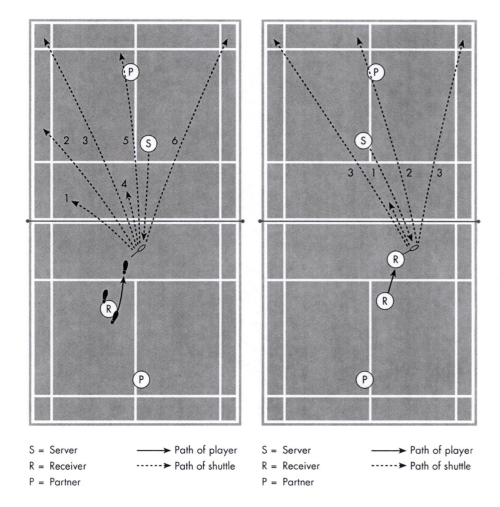

Figure 4.20 (on left)
Service returns hit from the "T" area in the odd court: (1) drop to side, (2) half-court, (3) drive, (4) drop to center, (5) drive to deep center, and (6) drive to cross-court back-court.

Figure 4.21 (on right)
Return of doubles serves directed at receiver's right shoulder: (1) straight-ahead drops, (2) drives at the server's partner, and (3) drives to the backcourt corners.

S = Server	⟶ Path of player
R = Receiver	┄┄► Path of shuttle
P = Partner	

S = Server	⟶ Path of player
R = Receiver	┄┄► Path of shuttle
P = Partner	

(shot 3). Because of the body positions and angles of shuttle flight, it is very difficult to hit accurate half-court service returns from this position.

    3. Returns of wide, short serves to the even court are depicted in Figure 4.22 (shots 1–5). Straight-ahead drops (shot 1), straight-ahead half-court drives (shot 2), and deep drives (shot 3) are all safe attacking shots. Drive returns into the body of the server's partner (shot 4) and half-court cross-court drives (shot 5) are also effective and give variety to the return.

These latter two shots require increased return skill and precise placement to be most effective.

    Returning the short serve with a clear gives the server the opportunity to gain the attack. This shot is not recommended unless the other returns described above are ineffective against your opponents.

    Drive serves should be returned with a drop or half-court shot down either sideline because these areas of the court are not easily defended (Figure 4.23). Other returns are risky because very little time is allowed to prepare for them. Returns for flick serves are depicted in Figure 4.24 (shots 1–4). Smashes into the body of the server who is moving to a side defensive position (shot 1), at the center line between the opponents (shot 2), or toward the straight-ahead sideline (shot 3) may be used. If the receiver is deceived or caught off-balance with the drive or flick serve, the safest return is a high deep clear (shot 4). After hitting drive or flick serves, many servers remain in the forecourt in hopes of smashing a drop shot service return. Thus, the drop shot return of the drive or flick serve could be risky unless the serving team moves to a side defensive position.

Figure 4.22 (on left)
Return of the doubles service directed at the receiver's sideline. (1) straight-ahead drops, (2) straight-ahead half-court drives, (3) straight-ahead drives to the backcourt, (4) drives to a server's partner, and (5) half-court cross-court drives.

Figure 4.23 (on right)
Return of doubles drive serves directed at the receiver's body: (1) drop shots to corners and (2) half-court smashes down either sideline.

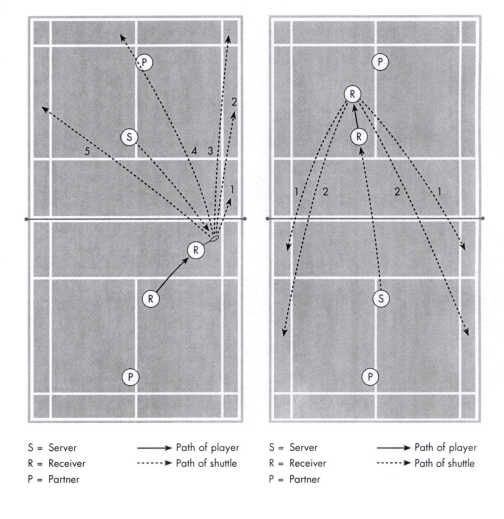

S = Server   → Path of player
R = Receiver   ----→ Path of shuttle
P = Partner

S = Server   → Path of player
R = Receiver   ----→ Path of shuttle
P = Partner

Doubles Offensive Strategy

When players are of equal ability, the team that maintains the attack (offense) will win about 60 percent to 70 percent of the rallies. The attacking formation is one in which one player moves to the backcourt in order to smash the cleared shuttle during which time his/her partner moves to midcourt to be positioned to attack a weak return. The players should move in tandem to position themselves in line with the flight of the most probable smash returns. The most effective positions are shown in Figure 4.25; there are two extremely important positions to note:

1. When the shuttle is smashed from near the sidelines, the forecourt player stays on the same side of the court as the smasher. This is necessary because an effectively smashed shuttle will generally be returned to this court position and moving to the cross-court position will allow an easy drop or block shot by the defender into the straight-ahead forecourt, which will also reverse the attack.

2. The forecourt player plays 3 to 6 feet behind the short service line. If the forecourt player is positioned in the area of the "T," very few shuttles are returned to this position; ones that do generally go past the player so fast that there isn't time to hit them. When the smasher is near the back boundary line, the forecourt player is deep (6 feet or more) behind the short service line (see a in Figure 4.25). If the smasher is in front of the long doubles service line, the forecourt player moves forward 3 to 4 feet (see b in Figure 4.25).

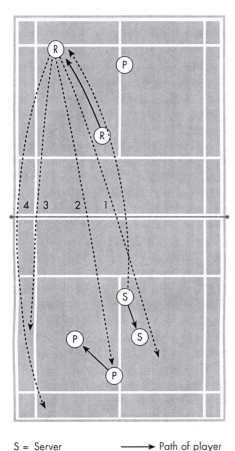

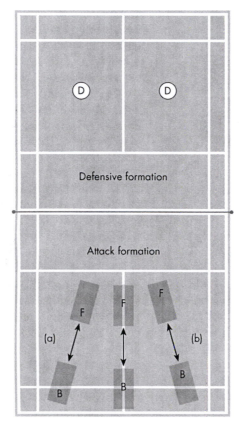

Defensive formation

Attack formation

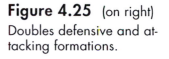

Figure 4.24 (on left)
Return of the doubles flick serve: (1) smashes at the server's body, (2) smashes between defenders, (3) straight-ahead smashes down the sideline, and (4) high, deep clears.

Figure 4.25 (on right)
Doubles defensive and attacking formations.

S = Server   ———▶ Path of player   F = Forecourt player   D = Defender
R = Receiver   ·····▶ Path of shuttle   B = Backcourt player   ———▶ Path of player
P = Partner

Figure 4.26

Smashing targets in doubles: (1) between center line and straight-ahead opponent, (2) straight-ahead sideline, and (3) sideline side of cross-court defender's body.

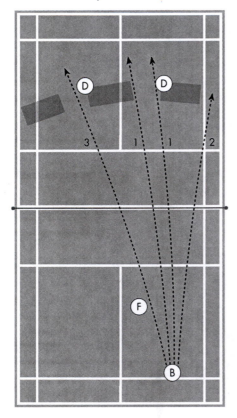

F = Forecourt player   D = Defender
B = Backcourt player   ------> Path of shuttle

This up-and-back position is only effective when the back-court player is able to smash the shuttle to one of the three primary target areas shown in Figure 4.26 (lines 1–3). The primary target (Figure 4.26, line 1) is directed between the center line and the body of the defensive player in front of the smasher. Since smash returns from this position are difficult to hit cross-court, the attacking team is lined up in tandem in the flight pattern of the anticipated smash return. The second target area is a steeply angled smash into the alley straight ahead (Figure 4.26, line 2). The shuttle smashed in this direction should be angled to hit the floor before it travels to the depth of the defensive player. The third target area is a hard and steeply angled smash directed at the body or right side of the cross-court defending player (Figure 4.26, line 3). Smash returns from the cross-court player are also generally returned in the direction of the forecourt attacker. This smash (line 3) is important because it keeps the cross-court defender positioned near the center of the even court, thus making it difficult for him/her to defend smashes directed down the center of the court.

The role of the backcourt player is to return all clear shots with smashes directed into the desired areas, attacking primarily the straight-ahead defender. The goal is to force a poor return, which the forecourt player can smash for a winning shot. Should the defending team return the smash with a hard drive, the backcourt player should try to drop the drive toward the center court so as to land between the defenders. Since this shot is also right in front of the forecourt player, the defenders must generally hit another clear, thus allowing the attackers to smash the next shuttle. Should the defender hit a drive and charge the net, the backcourt player (smasher) should be able to see this movement and hit a half-court shot past the charging player (generally toward the straight-ahead sideline).

The smasher's job is to keep smashing and moving the smash to various positions in the target areas until the defense hits a weak return or fails to retrieve the shuttle.

The role of the forecourt player is to keep in tandem with the backcourt player yet be in position to smash, to redrop the defensive player's drop, or to block returns for winners. The forecourt player should be as deep as possible in the court and be prepared to move forward or laterally toward the returned shuttle. Once the forecourt player gets into the rally, drives and smashes should be hit until the rally is won. If the defender hits a block or drop return that can't be smashed or driven, it is best to redrop the shuttle straight ahead. This will result in a clear, which the backcourt player can smash to maintain the attack. The most difficult shot for the forecourt player to return is the hard, low, flat drive return of a smash. The front-court player must avoid the temptation to hit this shot because there is a very high error factor and, more importantly, because this shot is quite easily returned by the backcourt player (who can then maintain control of the rally and keep the attack).

Should the defensive team return the smash with a cross-court drive, the smasher must cover this shot (Figure 4.27). This return is generally only possible when the smasher hits into poor lanes, as shown by the shaded areas in Figure 4.27. Since the front-court player is looking for a return from the target areas, he/she is generally slow to react to a cross-court return. The smasher, however, generally knows when a smash is misdirected and can immediately move cross-court even before the defenders return the smash. The smasher should either return this shot with a straight-ahead half-court (a in Figure 4.27) or use a drop shot to the center court area in order to regain the attack (b in Figure 4.27).

The forecourt player generally hits fewer shots than the backcourt player (smasher), but he/she must be ready to cut off a weak return and keep the attack with drives into the opponent's body and, finally, to hit a smash winner directed toward the center line.

If the shuttle is cleared in the center area of the court, the smashing team should direct shots down the center of the court or attack the defender's body. Defense is very difficult from the center of the court; almost any smash is safe, except for ones directed toward either sideline.

Maintaining the Attack

The smasher must strive to smash the shuttle with as steep an angle as possible so that the defenders retrieve the shuttle below their knees and thus must keep hitting the shuttle up in the air, which invites another smash.

The attackers should not smash if off-balance or out of position. A drop is the safer shot in this situation and can generally force another clear because the partner is in the forecourt to protect against a net shot.

Players who smash with a variety of speeds often upset their opponents' rhythm and thus make it more difficult for them to return the shuttle or reverse the attack.

Doubles Defensive Strategies

Although it is better to be on the attack, all players must know how to play defense. Since it is difficult to play winning badminton on the defense, the major defensive strategies discussed below will stress techniques to reverse (regain) the attack.

Playing defense consists of two important shots. The first is the lift or clear, allowing the opponent to hit a smash and take an offensive court position. Most often this will occur when a drop shot or half-court shot has to be retrieved from a low position (i.e., below knee level). The objectives of this clear are twofold:

1. Make the opponents smash from one of the baseline corners of the court. The defensive shot that reverses the attack can best be made when the opponent is forced to smash from the deep corners.

2. Force the smasher to hit the shuttle on the run. This tactic forces the smasher to hit a much more difficult shot, and any loss in accuracy will result in an easy defensive shot to reverse the attack. The defense is easier if the defender can be lined up to receive the smash from a backhand stroking position (e.g., a right-handed player defends the odd court from a straight-ahead smash).

The second shot of the defense is the reversal of the attack. The better the clear, the easier the reverse of attack becomes. The best defensive position is shown in Figure 4.28. It should be noted that, in this defensive position, the players are equidistant from the smasher with the cross-court player slightly closer to the net. If they are both right-handed players, almost all smash returns can be hit from the backhand stroking position. A basic rule here is that the cross-court player returns all shots down the middle, as shown in Figure 4.28. Thus, almost all shots are returned with the backhand stroke. If the shuttle were smashed from the deep even court, the situation would be reversed and all shots would be taken with forehand shots, which is a little more difficult for the defenders but has similar court coverage.

Figure 4.27

Cross-court drive smash defense and smasher's counter with (a) a shot straight ahead to half-court or (b) a drop shot to center court to regain the attack.

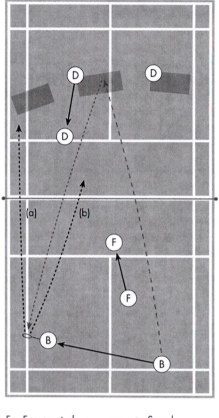

F = Forecourt player   – – –➤ Smash
B = Backcourt player   ------➤ Drive
D = Defender   ------➤ Smasher's counter

Figure 4.28 (on left)
Smash defensive position: Cross-court player covers smashes hit between defenders.

Figure 4.29 (center)
Doubles attack reversal with (1) a half-court straight-ahead drive, (2) a hard cross-court drive, or (3) a cross-court drop return of the smash to the defender's backhand.

Figure 4.30 (on right)
Forehand smash defense returns by the cross-court player to reverse the attack.

Reversing the Attack

The defensive players must try to reverse the attack by hitting a shot to a position that the offensive team cannot smash (Figure 4.29, shots 1–3). This generally means hitting a low flat drive, a half-court drive, or a drop shot. This is most easily achieved with a thumbs-up backhand grip for defense. The smash return should be a half-court straight-ahead drive (shot 1), a hard drive cross-court into the open court (shot 2), or a cross-court block near the service line (shot 3). All these shots will reverse the attack because the shuttle is directed with a low trajectory away from the forecourt player in the classic doubles attack formation. These shots will result in a clear by the attacking team, which means a complete reversal of the attack, or a series of drive and half-court shots, in which both sides will have an equal chance of hitting another shot to achieve the attack. In order to complete the reversal, the player hitting the half-court drive will follow the shuttle to the net, and his/her partner will move to the backcourt to assume the attacking position.

In the side-by-side defensive position, the player cross-court from the smasher should return most of the shuttles smashed from a deep corner between the defenders (Figure 4.30). Shots returned into the shaded court areas reverse the attack and biomechanically are the easiest for the defender to hit (see Figure 4.30). The player straight ahead of the shuttle defends the **back alley** and the shot directed at the body.

The defensive team should try to avoid the return of the smash with a clear because this return is generally not as well placed and the smasher won't have to run as far, thus giving the smasher a better chance to hit a winner or set up his/her part-

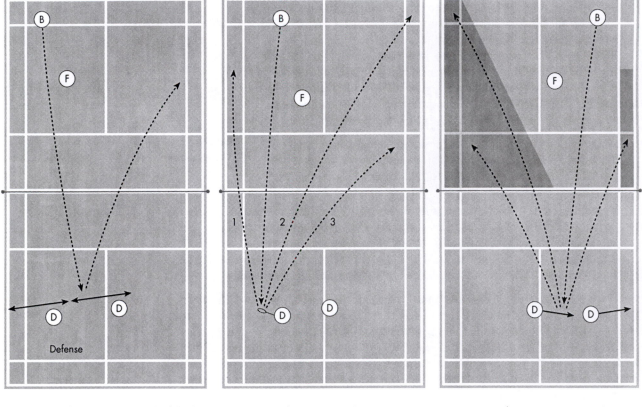

Defense

F = Forecourt player	----▶ Path of shuttle
B = Backcourt player	——▶ Path of Player
D = Defender	

F = Forecourt player	D = Defender
B = Backcourt player	----▶ Path of shuttle

F = Forecourt player	——▶ Path of player
B = Backcourt player	----▶ Path of shuttle
D = Defender	

ner at the net for a **put-away shot.** If the attacking player hits a drop instead of a smash, the best return is generally a clear to the opposite deep corner to make the attackers hit on the run. It also gives the defenders more time to get positioned and prepare for the drive and block return defense. If the smasher is already well positioned, clear the shuttle cross-court; then the smash will most likely be directed at your partner, who has much more time to prepare for the shot. If the smasher's partner stays deep in the court when a drop is made, the defender might be able to reverse the attack with a straight-ahead redrop.

If the clear is hit deep in the center of the court, the defensive team is at a significant disadvantage. The smasher has a much easier time attacking down the center area of the court, and the angles for the drive returns away from the smasher's partner are very difficult. This is one position in which an effective deep clear return of the smash to one of the corners might be one of the most appropriate returns. If a player in the forecourt is forced to hit a clear, he/she should back up and take a side-by-side defensive position.

Players should communicate with their partners to help them with line calls or to determine who is going to hit a shot directed between them. This can be achieved by calling "Out," "Yours," "Mine," "Hit," etc., as appropriate to the situation.

back alley The area between the back boundary line and the long service line for doubles.

put away A smash hit to win the rally.

Classic mixed doubles strategy uses the front-and-back attacking formation. In this formation, men play the power shots from the backcourt and women play the quick finesse and delicate net shots in the forecourt. The most effective shots in this formation are drives, half-court shots, and drops directed to either sideline. Players try not to hit clears because this formation leaves openings down either side for smashes.

Positioning of the players is such that the woman plays the forecourt near the doubles service line. Her primary movements are lateral, forward to the net, and somewhat deeper in the court toward the sidelines. She must return all drop shots; when she has good anticipation of the coming shot, she may return half-court shots and drives (Figure 4.31, shaded area). The male partner tries to establish a base position about 7 feet in from the back baseline (13 feet from the net) and is responsible for all power shots (hard drives, clears, attacking clears, and smashes) and many half-court shots.

MIXED DOUBLES STRATEGY

Mixed Doubles Service and Service Return Strategies

Service and service return positions are the same as for doubles when the woman is serving and returning the service. When the man is serving, he generally serves from about 6 feet behind the short service line. His partner should stand near the "T" (intersection of the center and short service lines) so as not to block the view of the opponent returning the serve (Figure 4.32). When serving from the odd court, a right-handed man often serves with his partner standing just to the left of the center line, as opposed to moving wide to the right and out of the play pattern (see F position in Figure 4.32). When the man is returning the service, the woman takes one of the three positions shown in Figure 4.33 (positions F1–F3), depending on the service return effectiveness and strategy of the teams. Position F1 is used when the service return is insufficient to allow the man time to get to the back of the court for the next shot. This is caused by either very good, low short services or minimum pressure exerted by the service return. Position F2 is used when the service return has good pressure but opponents are able to hit powerful cross-court drives, which can be returned better by the woman from this position than the man trying to recover positioning after the service return. Position F3 maintains the up-back attack and play position and is most effective when the man exerts extreme

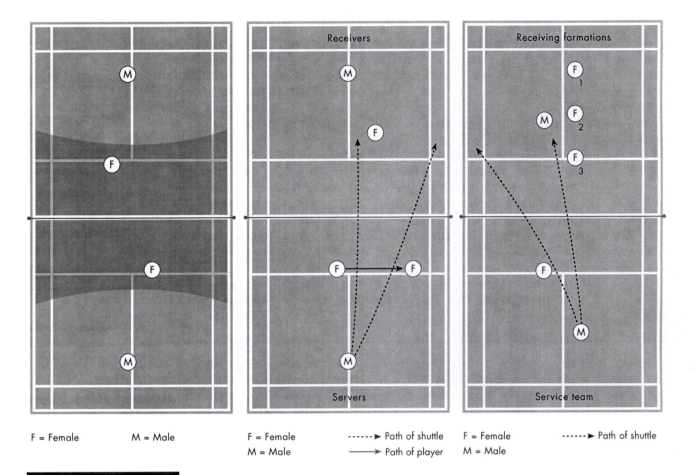

F = Female   M = Male

F = Female   ----▶ Path of shuttle
M = Male   ——▶ Path of player

F = Female   ----▶ Path of shuttle
M = Male

Figure 4.31 (on left)
In classic mixed doubles, the woman covers the forecourt (shaded area) and the man plays the backcourt.

Figure 4.32 (center)
Mixed doubles service position when the man is serving from the odd court.

Figure 4.33 (on right)
The woman's court positions when her partner is receiving service.

pressure with the quickness and placement of the service return. His service return must be forceful enough to prevent a deep return and/or he must be quick enough to cover the backcourt. Positions F1 and F2 have major disadvantages because the woman must work her way back to the forecourt, and her first shot is most likely to be in the forecourt corner that the man is trying to vacate. The man's return of service is one of the most crucial shots in mixed doubles.

When the woman serves or receives service, she stands in the same positions and hits the same serves and returns as she would use in women's doubles (review section titled The Doubles Serve).

Returning the Flick Service by the Woman

The most effective and safest service return of a flick service by the woman is a straight-ahead attacking drop or a steeply angled smash directed into the half-court area straight ahead (Figure 4.34). The basic idea is to hit a safe shot and get back to the forecourt position. This shot can be hit even when off-balance. The pace of her shot should be slow enough to provide time for her recovery and movement toward the forecourt because the shot doesn't have to be hit over or through an opponent. This shot is often a direct winner because both opponents have maximum distance to move and the speed is so quick that it is often perceived by the man to be coming farther back in the court where it could easily be returned.

Mixed doubles differs from singles and doubles events in that once a team is forced to hit a clear, which allows the opposition to hit a smash shot, the advantage shifts heavily in favor of the opponents. Because a smash is very difficult to defend against in mixed doubles, most teams will try to execute half-court drives and net shots at a higher risk level than in the other events in an attempt to avoid hitting clears. The half-court shot thus becomes the crucial shot in controlling the rally in mixed doubles.

Half-Court Shots

One of the most effective shots in mixed doubles is the half-court shot. This is a drive shot designed to clear the net as closely as possible and land in the opponent's court between 6 and 12 feet from the net (Figure 4.35). This shot is generally hit straight ahead when players are in good position and cross-court when the opponents are out of position. This shot is designed to pass by the forecourt player and then drop to the floor as quickly as possible. The primary effectiveness of this shot occurs when the shuttle has to be retrieved by the backcourt player after it has dropped to within about 1 foot of the floor. To retrieve the shuttle, the backcourt player must not only move toward the sideline but move forward in the court as well (see M in Figure 4.35). The woman will move toward the sideline and back toward midcourt to return the shuttle but may find that it gets past her (see Figure 4.35). The man usually gets a delayed start to retrieve this shot because he sees the woman's initial movement toward the shuttle. Unless the woman quickly moves back toward her base, she might get in her partner's way and obstruct him from hitting some shots. The placement of the half-court shot makes it very difficult for the opponent to return the shuttle with an attacking return. Thus, the opponent's shot selection is generally limited to straight-ahead half-court drives and net drops.

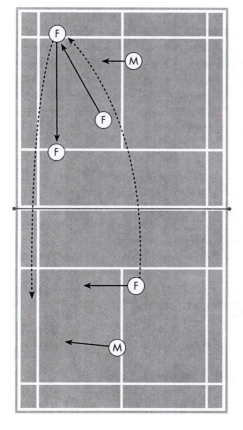

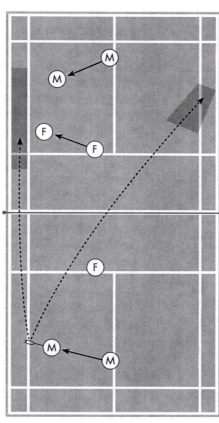

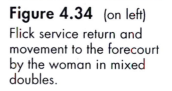

Figure 4.34 (on left)
Flick service return and movement to the forecourt by the woman in mixed doubles.

Figure 4.35 (on right)
Half-court shots in mixed doubles.

F = Female   ------▶ Path of shuttle
M = Male   ———▶ Path of player

F = Female   ———▶ Path of player
M = Male   ------▶ Path of shuttle

The Woman's Role in Mixed Doubles

Effective movement and positioning tactics, coupled with the basic serving and stroking skills by the woman, can provide the basis for a very formidable mixed doubles team. The woman should concentrate on the following three tactics:

1. *Prevent drop shot returns.* The woman should begin the match by assuming her opponent is going to hit a net drop on each shot. If a net drop is hit, the woman should attempt to catch the shuttle above the net and hit a smash or block shot to win the rally. Many players like to hit net drops on the service return; this must be prevented by the woman's using the above tactics, which will also score an easy point. The opponents would then adjust their losing tactics and greatly limit their frequency of net drops (especially on service returns). Once the woman controls the net by preventing drop shots, she can exert pressure on her opponents by anticipating and returning half-court shots.

2. *Move to the sidelines to cut off half-court shots.* Her goal is to anticipate and return the soft half-court shots with a straight-ahead half-court shot just past her opponent at the net. She should contact the shuttle at about net height or higher and direct it downward as steeply as possible. It is extremely important that the woman move to the same side of the court as the shuttle is directed. She must be in this position before her opponent hits the return. (An exception to this is when a clear has been hit and the opponent can smash the shuttle.) For example, if her opponent is hitting a shuttle from a deep sideline position, she should assume a position about halfway between the center line and the sideline on the same side of the court the returner is hitting from and be ready to move in any direction from this position (see F in Figure 4.36). From this position, soft half-court shots and net shots (Figure 4.36, shot 1) or cross-court drives (Figure 4.36, shot 2) can easily be attacked. Most importantly, this positioning strategy forces the opponent to hit a harder shot, which turns out to be a deep drive and not a half-court shot. Her partner now has many return options because he can hit the shuttle above waist level and attack the opponents (control the rally).

3. *Be alert and pick off a weak shot for the rally winner.* Once the woman has given her partner control of the rally by controlling the forecourt, she must be alert for the winning shot of the rally. She must keep moving to her position in front of the shuttle after each shot in the rally to prevent a reversal of the attack with a net drop or soft half-court shot. She must also be patient because it may take her partner several shots to force the weak return so that she can hit a winner. She should not attempt to return hard drives, even if they are within her reach, because her partner should be in a much better position to keep the attack by hitting steeply angled shots into the vacant areas of the opponents' court.

Mixed Doubles Smash Defense

Women generally take a cross-court defensive position using the frying pan (hammer) grip to defend against the smash. The racket head should be up, with the player positioning herself about one step behind the short service line. Very little swing is needed

Figure 4.36

Movement by the woman to stay on the same side of the court as the shuttle so as to cut off a half-court shot with (1) a straight-ahead half-court shot or (2) a cross-court drive.

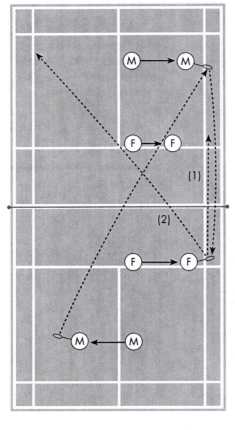

F = Female   ——▶ Path of player
M = Male   ┄┄┄▶ Path of shuttle

to block or drive the shuttle straight ahead into the open court (Figure 4.37). A weakness of this defense is that the attacker may hit either an attacking clear over the woman's head or a straight-ahead drop, both of which must be returned by the man, who is primarily looking for the smash. These two shots generally force weak returns and the attacking team can then smash through the defenders.

The players may elect to defend the smash from the front-and-back position if they can make the smasher hit on the run. This defense works if the smasher isn't able to hit with full power and accuracy into one of the alleys. In this defense, the man returns all smashes with straight-ahead half-court shots. If the smasher is off-balance getting to the shuttle and decides to hit a drop, the woman in the forecourt can usually smash it for a winning shot.

It is also possible to play the standard doubles side-by-side defense. In this defense, the woman usually defends in the cross-court position. The partners should try to reverse the attack after the first smash with a drive shot (as described in the section titled Doubles Strategy).

Communication and understanding are also important in mixed doubles. As in men's and women's doubles, mixed doubles players should call for shots to hit and help each other by calling "In" or "Out" for shots close to the boundary lines.

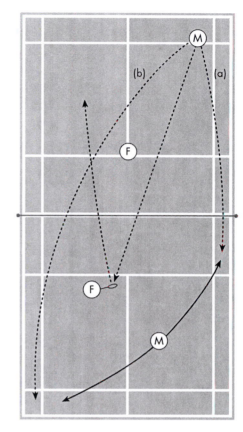

Figure 4.37

Mixed doubles smash defense.

F = Female   ———▶ Path of player
M = Male   ------▶ Path of shuttle

Glossary

Alley The 1.5-foot area of the court between the singles and doubles sidelines.

Around-the-head shot A stroke hit from the backhand side of the body with a forehand stroking pattern.

Attacking clear (offensive clear) A low, flat clear used to run the opponent to the backcourt.

Back alley The area between the back boundary line and the long service line for doubles.

Back boundary line (baseline) The end boundary of the court; also called the long service line for singles.

Backcourt The area between the center and the back boundary of the court.

Backhand A stroke hit on the opposite side of the body from the racket hand (e.g., left side of the body for right-handed players).

Backswing The initial part of a stroke in which the racket is taken back and the wrist cocked.

Base A ready position to which players try to return after each shot.

Baseline (back boundary line) The back boundary line of the court.

Bird (shuttle, shuttlecock) A slang term for a shuttle or shuttlecock, which is the object hit back and forth over the net.

Block shot A soft return of a smash requiring very little racket motion.

Carry (sling, throw) A shot in which the shuttle slides across the face of the racket and is misdirected from the intended shot (since 1981, this shot is legal if hit unintentionally).

Center line The line that divides the left and right service courts.

Clear (lob) A shot hit high and deep to the opponent's backcourt.

Combination doubles formation Partners play side-by-side on defense and up-and-back on offense.

Court The area marked by boundary lines for playing badminton.

Cross-court A shot hit diagonally from one side of the court to the other.

Cut shot (off-speed shot, slice) A shot in which the racket brushes across the shuttle at an angle to the direction of the swing in order to reduce shuttle speed and change the direction of the shuttle flight.

Deception Body or racket movement used to lead the receiver to believe the shuttle will be hit at a different speed or direction than it actually is.

Defense A situation in which the opponent has the opportunity to hit a smash.

Double hit In singles, one player hitting the shuttle twice in succession, or in doubles, both players hitting the shuttle during the same shot; it is a fault.

Doubles A game played with two players on each side.

Doubles service court The area to which a serve must be delivered in doubles events.

Down-the-line shot A drive shot directed straight ahead down the sideline.

Drive A sidearm stroke hit so as to land between the opponent's short service line and the back boundary line.

Drive serve A hard and quickly hit service with a flat trajectory.

Drop shot (drop) A shot hit from any position that passes close to the net and lands in the opponent's front court (in front of the short service line).

Even court The side of the court corresponding with the right service court.

Face The strung surface of the racket.

Fault A violation of the rules. See Law 14.

First server A term in doubles indicating that the player serving is the first server of that inning.

Flick serve A service hit with a trajectory to just pass over the receiver's outstretched racket and land near the long service line.

Follow-through Movement of the racket and the player's body after racket–shuttle contact during the execution of a shot.

Foot fault Illegal placement or movement of a player's foot during the service. See Law 14c.

Footwork Foot movement patterns used to move about the court.

Forecourt The area between the net and the center of the court.

Forehand Strokes hit on the racket side of the body.

Frying pan grip A variation of the forehand grip, used primarily for net play when the shuttle is above the level of the net.

Game A badminton game is played to 15 points in all events except women's singles, which is played to 11 points, unless the game has been "set." See Rule 7; Scoring.

Game point A designation to indicate that the rally ends the game if it is won by the server.

Grip The covering, usually leather, of the racket handle; the positioning of the hand holding the racket handle.

Half-court shot A shot hit down the sideline that lands in the opponent's court midway between the net and the back baseline.

Hand in (see First server)

International Badminton Federation (IBF) Governing body for international competition.

Inning The period during which a player or team holds the service.

Kill (put-away, winner) A smash hit to win the rally.

Let An incident that requires the replay of a rally. See Rules 12 and 17.

Lob (see Clear)

Long serve A high serve directed toward the receiver's back boundary line.

Love A term used to indicate a score of zero points.

Match The best two out of three games.

Match point A rally that if won by the server ends the match.

Mixed doubles A game contested with a male and a female on each team.

Net shot A shot played to the opponent's forecourt that drops close to the net.

Net tape The white strip marking the top of the net.

Odd court The side of the court corresponding with the left service court.

Offense A player or team that's on the attack or that has the opportunity to smash the shuttle.

Off-speed shot (see Cut shot, Slice)

Out A term used by a player or line judge to indicate the shuttle landed out of court.

Overhead Strokes hit above head height.

Power shots Shots that are hit very hard (e.g., clears, drives, and smashes).

Pronation The inward rotation of the forearm, primarily used in forehand strokes.

Push shot A soft shot hit with little racket motion from the forecourt to the opponent's forecourt or midcourt; often used to hit doubles service returns.

Put away (see Kill)

Racket An implement used to strike the shuttle.

Racket foot (racket leg) The foot or leg on the side of the body at which the racket is held (e.g., the right foot or leg for a right-handed player).

Rally The exchange of shots during play or during warm-up.

Ready position (see Base)

Receiver The player who receives the service.

Rush the serve A doubles service return tactic to move quickly to attack the opponent's low serve.

Second server A term used in doubles to indicate that the server is the second player to serve in that inning.

Server The player who hits the serve.

Service The act of putting the shuttle into play to begin a rally.

Service court The singles or doubles court boundary into which the service must be delivered.

Service over A term meaning the other side gains the service.

Setting A method of extending the game when the score is tied near the end of the game. See Rule 7.

Setup A shot that gives the opponent an easy chance to win the rally.

Shaft The part of the racket connecting the handle and the head.

Short serve A serve hit just over the net to land near the short service line; used as the primary serve in doubles.

Short service line The forecourt boundary line over which the service must pass.

Shot A clear, drive, drop, or smash that has been hit from one of the stroking positions.

Shuttle (bird, shuttlecock) The object hit back and forth over the net.

Shuttlecock (bird, shuttle) The object hit back and forth over the net.

Side-by-side formation A doubles defensive formation in which the players play side by side in midcourt.

Slice (see Cut shot, Off-speed shot)

Sling (see Carry)

Smash A hard overhand shot hit with a downward angle.

Split-step A footwork movement pattern taken just as the opponent is striking the shuttle to provide dynamic stability for quick movement in any direction.

Stroke The basic hitting pattern from which all shots are executed.

Supination The outward rotation of the forearm, primarily used in backhand strokes.

"T" The area of the court near the intersection of the short service line and the center line.

Thomas Cup An international men's team competition held every 2 years.

Toss Before a match begins, players toss a coin, spin a racket, or hit a shuttle to determine who will serve or defend from which court end.

Trajectory The flight pattern of the shuttle.

Uber Cup An international women's team competition held every 2 years.

Underhand Strokes in which the shuttle is contacted below the waist and in front of the body.

USA Badminton The national governing body for badminton in the United States.

Up-and-back formation A doubles formation providing the best attack positioning; the classic mixed doubles positioning has the woman in the forecourt and the man in the backcourt.

Winner (see Kill, Put-away)

Index

Breinigsville, PA USA
30 November 2009
228340BV00003B/10/P